Chef
express

fresh
appetizers

table of contents

introduction

Perfect with drinks when getting together with friends, for snacks while watching a movie or on family picnics, even when improvising a fast lunch or light supper, these finger foods are a magic resource for cooks on the spot. To serve and enjoy them, keep in mind these basic guidelines.

fresh appetizers
introduction

- In all cases, the presentation and cutting of vegetables and meats for appetizers should be meticulous.
- Cheeses, spread sauces like mayonnaise, aioli (garlic mayonnaise), eggplant caviar (smashed eggplant with garlic and olive oil), tapenade (paste of olives and anchovies), pâtés, salmon and avocado are some essential ingredients.
- To accelerate the preparation to maximum speed, it's best to choose some original snow-pea boats or an all time classic like guacamole.
- Foccacias and toasts or grilled breads go well with spread pastes and can be topped with eggs in quarters, chopped olives, pan-fried slices of spring onions, or whatever your imagination may suggest.

- Pan-frying, the fast cooking technique par excellence, offers options as simple as carrot meatballs, or as sophisticated as cheese cigars with cilantro pesto.
- More complex and subtle are the potato skins with different toppings or the zucchini filled with pork, ginger and cayenne pepper.
- Those who can spare a couple of hours to marinate delights can try lamb and mango kebabs or spicy Indian-style chicken.
- Blue cheese, Parmesan, onion and sesame seed crackers are a complete option in themselves, the same as polenta cups filled with meat and beans.
- Other veggie varieties are easy eggplant and mozzarella cakes or fancy spinach and cheese mini quiches.

Difficulty scale

■□□ I Easy to do

■■□ I Requires attention

■■■ I Requires experience

snow pea boats with minted cream cheese

■■□ I Cooking time: 1 minute - Preparation time: 35 minutes

ingredients

> **18 snow peas, trimmed**
> **125 g/4 oz cream cheese**
> **30 g/1 oz butter**
> **60 g/2 oz fresh mint leaves, finely chopped**
> **1 teaspoon sugar**
> **1 teaspoon horseradish relish**

method

1. Drop snow peas into a saucepan of boiling water (a) and cook for 1 minute. Drain and refresh under cold running water. Pat dry on absorbent paper.
2. Beat cream cheese and butter together until smooth. Add mint, sugar and horseradish. Slit snow peas along one edge (b) with a sharp knife or scissors. Spoon or pipe cream cheese mixture into snow peas (c). Refrigerate until firm.

....
Serves 6

tip from the chef
Snow peas are edible pea pods. To prepare for cooking, top and tail with a sharp knife and pull away strings from older, larger peas. Snow peas can be steamed, boiled, microwaved or stir-fried.

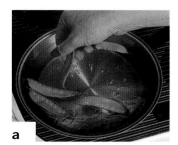

a

b

c

cherry tomatoes with parmesar

nd rosemary

■□□ | Cooking time: 1 minute - Preparation time: 25 minutes

method

1. Sprinkle the inside of tomatoes with black pepper.
2. In a small bowl, combine cheese, cream, nutmeg and rosemary, mix well.
3. Spoon mixture into the tomatoes and grill for 1 minute. Serve immediately.

....

Serves 4

ingredients

> **1 punnet cherry tomatoes, halved and seeded**
> **black pepper**
> **¹/4 cup grated Parmesan cheese**
> **1 tablespoon cream**
> **pinch nutmeg**
> **1 tablespoon fresh rosemary, finely chopped**

tip from the chef

When buying tomatoes for being stuffed, choose those that are firm and even-sized.

guacamole
with corn chips

■□□ | Cooking time: 1/2 minute - Preparation time: 25 minutes

ingredients

> **3 avocados**
> **2 small tomatoes**
> **1 small onion, very finely chopped**
> **3 red chilies, chopped**
> **2 tablespoons fresh coriander, chopped**
> **2 tablespoons lemon juice**
> **2 x 200 g/6¹/₂ oz packets corn chips**

method

1. Cut avocados in half, remove stone (a) and skin (b). Mash roughly with a fork.
2. Plunge tomatoes into boiling water for 30 seconds, remove. Peel off skin, cut into quarters, remove and discard seeds. Cut tomatoes into small dice (c).
3. Combine avocado, tomato, onion, chili, coriander and lemon juice (d). Serve with corn chips for dipping.

Serves 8

tip from the chef
The famous Mexican specialty is also delicious served as a side dish for grilled meats.

a

b

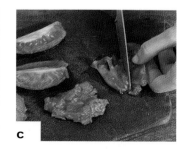

c

d

artichoke
savories

■□□ | Cooking time: 10-15 minutes - Preparation time: 25 minutes

method

1. Using a 5 cm/2 in biscuit cutter, cut out 12 circles of bread. Brush both sides of each bread circle with a little oil and place on a baking tray lined with nonstick baking paper and bake at 200°C/400°F/Gas 6 for 10-15 minutes or until bread is golden and toasted.
2. Place mayonnaise, cream, chives and black pepper to taste in a small bowl and mix to combine.
3. To assemble, top each bread circle with half an artichoke heart, a spoonful of mayonnaise mixture, a little red pepper and a sprig of dill. Serve immediately.

ingredients

> **12 slices bread**
> **3 tablespoons vegetable oil**
> **¼ cup/60 g/2 oz mayonnaise**
> **1 tablespoon cream (double)**
> **1 tablespoon snipped fresh chives**
> **freshly ground black pepper**
> **2 tablespoons finely chopped red pepper**
> **440 g/14 oz canned artichoke hearts, drained and halved**
> **12 sprigs fresh dill**

....
Makes 12

tip from the chef

For these savories, the toast rounds and the mayonnaise can be made in advance, but leave the assembly until just prior to serving or the toast will go soggy.

smoked
salmon bagels

■□□ | Cooking time: 0 minutes - Preparation time: 25 minutes

ingredients

> **4 bagels, split**
> **125 g/4 oz cream cheese, softened**
> **2 tablespoons snipped fresh chives**
> **250 g/8 oz smoked salmon slices**
> **1 onion, thinly sliced**
> **1 avocado, stoned, peeled and sliced**
> **1 tablespoon capers, drained**
> **1 tablespoon lemon juice**

method

1. Spread each bagel half with cream cheese and sprinkle with chives. Top bagel halves with salmon, onion, avocado and capers. Sprinkle with lemon juice and serve immediately.

....

Serves 4

tip from the chef

A tomato and onion salad is a delicious side dish. To make salad, arrange sliced tomatoes and very thinly sliced onion on a lettuce-lined dish. Sprinkle with chopped fresh basil and drizzle with French dressing. Season to taste with black pepper.

greek
tuna focaccia

■□□ I Cooking time: 5 minutes - Preparation time: 20 minutes

method

1. Split focaccia bread horizontally and toast lightly under a preheated medium grill.
2. Top each piece of bread with feta cheese, rocket or watercress, tuna, sun-dried tomatoes, capers and onion rings. Sprinkle with dill.

....

Serves 4

ingredients

- > **2 x 10 cm/4 in squares focaccia bread**
- > **90 g/3 oz marinated or plain feta cheese, crumbled**
- > **1/2 bunch rocket or watercress, broken into sprigs**
- > **440 g/14 oz canned tuna in brine or springwater, drained**
- > **60 g/2 oz sun-dried tomatoes in oil, drained and sliced**
- > **1 tablespoon capers, drained**
- > **1 onion, thinly sliced into rings**
- > **1 tablespoon chopped fresh dill**

tip from the chef

Another variation is to make a paste with cooked fish, black olives, cream cheese and fresh coriander. Spread on toasted bread, garnish with thinly sliced spring onions.

egg and onion spirals

■□□ I Cooking time: 0 minutes - Preparation time: 20 minutes

ingredients

> **1 loaf unsliced wholemeal bread**
> **125 g/4 oz butter, softened**

egg and spring onion filling

> **8 hard-boiled eggs**
> **4 spring onions, finely chopped**
> **2 tablespoons mayonnaise**
> **2 tablespoons sour cream**
> **2 teaspoons dry mustard**

method

1. To make filling, place eggs in a bowl and mash. Add spring onions, mayonnaise, sour cream and mustard and mix well to combine.
2. Butter the bread and spread filling over it evenly with a spatula. Roll up tightly, wrap in plastic film and chill until firm. Remove from fridge, unwrap and slice.

············

Makes 25

tip from the chef
These rolls are delicious when matched with a chilled, slightly sparkling Chardonnay wine.

classic
bruschetta

■□□ I Cooking time: 3 minutes - Preparation time: 10 minutes

method

1. Grill ciabatta slices on each side for 2-3 minutes.
2. Brush with olive oil, spread with sun-dried tomato paste, then top with bocconcini slices and shredded basil leaves, or whole leaves.

....

Serves 6

ingredients

> **1 ciabatta loaf, cut in 1½ cm/½ in slices**
> **60 ml/2 fl oz olive oil**
> **½ cup/80 g/2½ oz sun-dried tomato paste**
> **180 g/6 oz bocconcini, each ball shredded into 5 slices**
> **½ cup/45 g/1½ oz basil leaves, shredded, or whole leaves**

tip from the chef

Ciabatta is an Italian bread made from pizza dough: 450 g/1 lb flour, 15 g/½ oz fresh yeast, a pinch of sugar, 1 teaspoon salt and 4 tablespoons olive oil.

herb
liver pâté

■□□ | Cooking time: 12 minutes - Preparation time: 35 minutes

ingredients

> **185 g/6 oz butter, softened**
> **1 onion, chopped**
> **2 cloves garlic, chopped**
> **2 tablespoons fresh thyme leaves**
> **1 tablespoon fresh rosemary leaves**
> **750 g/1¹/2 lb fresh chicken livers, cleaned and trimmed, coarsely chopped**
> **pinch salt**
> **freshly ground black pepper**
> **75 g/2¹/2 oz melba toasts or rice crackers**
> **125 g/4 oz stuffed green olives, sliced**

method

1. Melt 60 g/2 oz of the butter in a frying pan over a low heat, add onion, garlic, thyme and rosemary and cook, stirring, for 6-8 minutes or until onion is very tender.
2. Add livers to pan, increase heat to medium and cook, stirring, until livers are brown on the outside, but still pink in the center. Set aside to cool.
3. Place liver mixture in a food processor, add remaining butter, salt and black pepper to taste and process until smooth. Spoon mixture into a piping bag fitted with a large star nozzle and pipe rosettes onto melba toasts or rice crackers. Arrange on a serving plate, garnish with olive slices and serve.

Makes about 30

tip from the chef
The secret of these tidbits is to present them topping crisp thin crackers or pumpernickel slices.

tuna melts

■□□ | Cooking time: 7 minutes - Preparation time: 25 minutes

method

1. Sauté the onion in the butter till soft and golden. Add the drained tuna, salt, pepper and Tabasco. Stir to mix ingredients and to flake the tuna. Allow to cool.
2. Place a teaspoonful of mixture on each water cracker biscuit. Cut each cheese slice into strips. Place a few strips over tuna mixture on each biscuit.
3. Cut a slice of gherkin and place on top. Set under hot grill until cheese melts and the tuna mixture is covered.

ingredients

> **1 small onion, finely chopped**
> **2 teaspoons butter**
> **185 g/6$^1/_4$ oz canned tuna in oil, drained**
> **salt and pepper**
> **$^1/_4$ teaspoon Tabasco**
> **16 water cracker biscuits**
> **4 sandwich cheese slices**
> **2 sweet gherkins**

....

Serves 4

tip from the chef

To avoid soda crackers from getting soft, prepare tidbits right before serving.

cheese cigars
with coriander pesto

■■□ | Cooking time: 10 minutes - Preparation time: 30 minutes

ingredients

> **12 slices white sandwich bread, crusts removed**
> **2 teaspoons prepared English mustard**
> **4 tablespoons finely grated fresh Parmesan cheese**
> **1/2 cup grated mozzarella cheese**
> **1 tablespoon snipped fresh chives**
> **cayenne pepper**
> **1 egg, lightly beaten**
> **vegetable oil for cooking**

coriander pesto

> **3 large bunches fresh coriander**
> **2 cloves garlic, crushed**
> **60 g/2 oz pine nuts**
> **1/2 cup/120 ml/4 fl oz olive oil**
> **2/3 cup grated fresh Parmesan cheese**

method

1. Roll each slice of bread with a rolling pin, to flatten as much as possible.
2. Combine mustard, Parmesan cheese, mozzarella cheese, chives and cayenne pepper to taste in a bowl. Divide mixture between bread slices and spread over half of each bread slice. Brush unspread sides of bread slices with egg. Roll each slice up tightly using the egg to seal rolls. Arrange side by side on a tray. Cover and refrigerate until ready to cook.
3. Heat 2 cm/3/4 inch oil in a skillet. When hot, cook cigars a few at a time until evenly golden all over. Drain on paper towels.
4. To make pesto, place coriander leaves, garlic and pine nuts in a food processor or blender and process until finely chopped. With machine running slowly, pour in oil and process mixture until smooth. Add cheese and process to blend. Serve with hot cigars.

Makes 12

tip from the chef

A pesto made of coriander is the accompaniment to these tasty cheese cigars — serve as an indulgent snack or as a pre-dinner treat.

carrot balls

a

■ ■ □ | Cooking time: 5 minutes - Preparation time: 45 minutes

method

1. Place carrots, orange rind, Swiss cheese, Parmesan cheese, mint, black pepper to taste and half the egg mixture in a bowl (a) and mix to combine. Shape carrot mixture into balls.

2. Place bran and almonds in a bowl and mix to combine. Roll balls in flour, then dip in remaining egg mixture and roll in bran mixture (b). Place balls on a plate lined with plastic food wrap and refrigerate for 30 minutes.

3. Heat oil in a large saucepan until a cube of bread dropped in browns in 50 seconds (c). Cook balls, a few at a time, for 4-5 minutes or until golden (d) and heated through. Drain on absorbent kitchen paper and serve immediately.

ingredients

> 3 carrots, grated
> 2 teaspoons orange rind
> 60 g/2 oz grated Swiss cheese
> 60 g/2 oz grated Parmesan cheese
> 1 tablespoon chopped fresh mint
> freshly ground black pepper
> 2 eggs, lightly beaten
> 1 cup/30 g/1 oz unprocessed bran
> 3 tablespoons finely chopped almonds
> flour
> vegetable oil for deep-frying

....

Serves 4

tip from the chef

These carrot balls make for great starters when served with a green salad.

b

c

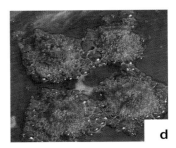
d

cheese puffs

■■□ | Cooking time: 5 minutes - Preparation time: 30 minutes

ingredients

> **4 cups/500 g/1 lb grated tasty cheese**
> **1 cup/90 g/3 oz fresh breadcrumbs**
> **4 eggs, separated**
> **1 teaspoon dry mustard**
> **1 teaspoon paprika**
> **salt and pepper**
> **fresh breadcrumbs, extra**
> **oil for deep frying**

method

1. Combine cheese, breadcrumbs, egg yolks, mustard, paprika, salt and pepper (a). Mix well.
2. Beat egg whites until stiff. Gently fold into the cheese mixture (b).
3. Shape mixture into small, walnut sized, balls. Roll in extra breadcrumbs (c).
4. Deep fry, a few at a time (d), until golden brown, about 30 seconds.

Serves 4

tip from the chef
Serve them real hot, using small skewers.

a

b

c

d

potato
croquettes

a

■■□ | Cooking time: 40 minutes - Preparation time: 30 minutes

method

1. Place potatoes in a saucepan of water and bring to the boil. Reduce heat, cover and simmer for 20-25 minutes or until potatoes are cooked. Drain potatoes and press through a sieve into a bowl.

2. Add breadcrumbs, spring onions, cottage cheese, egg, parsley, oregano and black pepper to taste to potatoes (a) and mix to combine. Cover and refrigerate until potato mixture is cold.

3. Divide potato mixture into 12 portions and shape into croquettes. Roll each croquette in flour (b) and place on a plate lined with plastic food wrap.

4. Heat oil in a large saucepan until a cube of bread dropped in browns in 50 seconds. Cook a few croquettes at a time for 4-5 minutes (c) or until golden and heated through. Drain on absorbent kitchen paper and serve immediately.

ingredients

> **500 g/1 lb potatoes, cut into quarters**
> **100 g/3¹/₂ oz wholemeal breadcrumbs**
> **4 spring onions, chopped**
> **250 g/8 oz cottage cheese**
> **1 egg, lightly beaten**
> **1 tablespoon chopped fresh parsley**
> **1 tablespoon chopped fresh oregano or 1 teaspoon dried oregano**
> **freshly ground black pepper**
> **1¹/₂ cups/230 g/7¹/₂ oz wholemeal flour**
> **vegetable oil for deep-frying**

....
Serves 4

b

c

tip from the chef

Potato croquettes make an interesting alternative to plain potatoes when served as an accompaniment. They are also a delicious light meal, served with salad and mango chutney.

baby squash with pepper and cheese filling

■■□ | Cooking time: 20 minutes - Preparation time: 40 minutes

ingredients

> **24 yellow baby squash**
> **1 large red pepper, finely chopped**
> **1/2 cup/60 g/2 oz tasty cheese (mature Cheddar), grated**
> **1 egg, lightly beaten**
> **2 spring onions, finely chopped**
> **1/4 teaspoon cayenne pepper**

method

1. Cook squash in boiling water until tender, drain, cool. Scoop out top part of each squash.
2. Combine red pepper, cheese, egg, spring onions and cayenne pepper. Spoon into squash.
3. Bake at 180°C/350°F/Gas 4 for 10 minutes or until heated through.

Makes 24

tip from the chef

These nice baby squash can also be stuffed with a three cheese mix (blue, cream and cottage), ham and chopped onions. Then, gratin in oven.

ginger
pork zucchini

▪▪☐ | Cooking time: 25 minutes - Preparation time: 45 minutes

method

1. Wash the zucchini and cut them into 8 cm/3 in pieces. With a small sharp knife hollow out the center by removing all the seeds, being careful not to pierce the skin.
2. Put the zucchini pieces in a pot of boiling water and cook them on high heat for 3 minutes. Drain them, run them under cold water and set them aside.
3. In a large frying pan melt the butter and sauté the onion and garlic until golden in color. Do not brown them. Add the meat and cook the mixture over high heat for about 10 minutes or until the meat is completely cooked.
4. Drain on paper towels. Put the meat mixture in a food processor and add all other ingredients. Process until mixture is finely ground.
5. Carefully stuff the zucchini with the filling until firmly packed. Refrigerate them until ready to use. At serving time heat the stuffed pieces for 5-8 minutes in oven, preheated at 180°C/350°F/Gas 4. Slice them and serve immediately.

....
Makes 36 slices

ingredients

> **6 medium zucchini**

gingered pork filling

> **1 tablespoon butter**
> **2 medium onions, chopped**
> **2 cloves garlic, chopped**
> **350 g/12 oz minced pork**
> **1/2 teaspoon ground ginger**
> **1/2 teaspoon cayenne pepper**
> **1 tablespoon tomato paste**
> **1 tablespoon dry white wine**
> **1/8 teaspoon salt**
> **dash pepper**

tip from the chef

Ginger and pork meat make a good match. Both strong and temperamental, they balance each other.

cheese
and chive cookies

■ ■ □ | Cooking time: 10 minutes - Preparation time: 45 minutes

ingredients

> **1 cup/125 g/4 oz self-raising flour, sifted**
> **125 g/4 oz butter, cut into pieces**
> **60 g/2 oz hard blue cheese, crumbled**
> **2 tablespoons grated Parmesan cheese**
> **3 tablespoons snipped fresh chives**
> **4 tablespoons sesame seeds**

method

1. Place flour, butter, blue and Parmesan cheeses and chives in a food processor and process until ingredients cling together. Turn onto a lightly floured surface and knead lightly. Shape dough into a ball, wrap in plastic food wrap and chill for 30 minutes.
2. Roll heaped teaspoons of mixture into balls, then roll in sesame seeds to coat. Place balls on lightly greased baking trays, flatten slightly with a fork and bake at 220°C/425°F/Gas 7 for 10 minutes or until golden. Stand on trays for 3 minutes, then transfer to wire racks to cool. Store cookies in an airtight container.

Makes 30

tip from the chef

These nutritious crackers should always be served at the beginning of a meal or to complement lighter preparations and vegetables.

chili
bean corn cups

a

■■■ | Cooking time: 90 minutes - Preparation time: 45 minutes

method

1. To make pastry, place butter and cream cheese in a small bowl (a) and mix to combine. Make a ring with flour, polenta and salt; pour the previous mixture into the center and blend together to form a soft dough. Turn dough onto a lightly floured surface (b) and knead until smooth. Divide dough into small balls, press into lightly greased muffin tins (c) and bake at 180°C/350°F/Gas 4 for 20 minutes or until golden.

2. Heat oil in a frying pan over a medium heat, add onion and garlic and cook, stirring, for 5 minutes or until onion is tender. Add beef, cumin and chili powder and stir-fry for 4-5 minutes or until beef is brown.

3. Stir in tomatoes and beans and bring to the boil. Reduce heat and simmer, stirring occasionally, for 1 hour or until most of the liquid evaporates and mixture is quite dry. Season to taste with black pepper and spoon into hot polenta cups. Serve immediately.

ingredients

> 2 tablespoons vegetable oil
> 1 large onion, chopped
> 2 cloves garlic, crushed
> 250 g/8 oz lean beef mince
> 2 teaspoons ground cumin
> 2 teaspoons chili powder
> 440 g/14 oz canned peeled tomatoes, undrained and mashed
> 440 g/14 oz canned red kidney beans, drained and rinsed
> freshly ground black pepper

polenta pastry
> 185 g/6 oz butter
> 185 g/6 oz cream cheese
> 2 cups/250 g/8 oz flour
> 1 cup/170 g/5^1/2 oz polenta
> pinch salt

Makes 24

tip from the chef
Other options for filling: pan-fried ground meat with onions and thyme, mashed eggplant with garlic and olive oil, goat cheese with chopped tomatoes.

b

c

curried
sausage puffs

■■□ | Cooking time: 18 minutes - Preparation time: 35 minutes

ingredients

> **2 sheets ready-rolled puff pastry**
> **375 g/³/4 lb sausage mince**
> **1 small carrot, finely grated**
> **2 spring onions, chopped**
> **1 tablespoon fruit chutney**
> **1 teaspoon curry powder**
> **salt and pepper**

method

1. Cut pastry sheets in half.
2. Combine mince, carrot, spring onions, chutney and curry powder (a), season to taste with salt and pepper, divide into 4, roll each into a sausage shape (b) the length of the long side of the pastry.
3. Place sausage along pastry, roll up, and seal edge with water. Cut roll into 1 cm/¹/2 in slices (c).
4. Place slices onto greased baking tray; bake at 200°C/400°F/Gas 6 for 15 minutes or until golden brown and puffed.

....
Makes 24

tip from the chef
This filling can be used to make baby phyllo pastry parcels.

a

b

c

potato skins

■ ■ □ | Cooking time: 40 minutes - Preparation time: 50 minutes

method

1. Preheat the oven at 180°C/350°F/Gas 4.
Wash and dry each potato. Pierce with a
fork and place in the preheated oven. Bake
for 30 minutes or until the center is firm
but can be easily pierced with a fork.
2. Cool the potato, cut in quarters lengthwise
and cut out the center leaving the skin with
0.5 cm/¼ in to 110 mm/½ in of potato on it.
3. Brush the skins with butter, then sprinkle
them with salt and pepper. Bake for
10 minutes. Top them with chosen topping
and bake for another 5-10 minutes until
warmed.

Makes 4 pieces per potato

ingredients

> baking potatoes

bacon and mushroom topping

> potato pulp
> sautéed bacon and mushroom
> parsley

shrimp and chives topping

> potato pulp
> sour cream
> chopped fresh chives
> shrimps
> salt and pepper to taste

chicken and almond topping

> potato pulp
> cooked chicken
> toasted pine nuts
> chopped shallots
> sour cream
> black pepper

tip from the chef

*Topping preparations are also good for filling
pastry cases made with 175 g/6 oz flour, a
pinch of salt, 90 g/3 oz refrigerated butter,
1 egg yolk and 1 tablespoon water.*

mini spinach and cheese quiches

■ ■ □ | Cooking time: 20 minutes - Preparation time: 35 minutes

ingredients

> **3 sheets ready-rolled puff pastry**
> **125 g/4¹/₂ oz tasty cheese (mature Cheddar), cubed**
> **2 spinach leaves, washed and torn into large strips, with stems removed**
> **¹/₂ small onion, peeled and halved**
> **1 egg**
> **3 tablespoons cream**
> **1 tablespoon parsley sprigs, firmly packed**
> **1 tablespoon French mustard**
> **salt, pepper**

method

1. Cut pastry into 6 cm/2¹/₂ in rounds with a pastry cutter and press into shallow patty pans.
2. In a food processor, process the cheese, spinach, onion, egg, cream, parsley, mustard, salt and pepper until all ingredients are finely chopped and well combined.
3. Spoon 1 tablespoon of mixture into each patty pan.
4. Bake at 200°C/400°F/Gas 6 for 20 minutes, or until puffed and golden.
5. Remove from pans, place on platter and serve.

. . . .
Makes about 24

tip from the chef

Variations
- *Crab and ham: Substitute for cheese, spinach and parsley with 170 g/6 oz canned crab meat, drained, and 125 g/4¹/₂ oz sliced ham.*
- *Cheese and ham: Substitute for spinach leaves with 125 g/4¹/₂ oz sliced ham.*

eggplant with mozzarella cheese

■ □ □ | Cooking time: 9 minutes - Preparation time: 10 minutes

method

1. Lightly brush eggplant slices with combined oil, garlic and pepper. Grill until lightly browned, approximately 3 minutes each side.
2. Top each slice with mozzarella cheese and decorate with pimento strips.
3. Return to the grill and cook until cheese has melted. Serve immediately and garnish with fresh basil if desired.

ingredients

> **1 medium eggplant, cut into 1 cm/$1/2$ in slices**
> **3 tablespoons olive oil**
> **1 clove garlic, crushed**
> **$1/4$ teaspoon pepper**
> **8 thin slices mozzarella cheese**
> **2 pimentos, sliced into strips**
> **fresh basil (optional)**

....
Makes 8

tip from the chef

With eggplant you can make a dressing that goes with everything: the so-called caviar. To prepare, roast eggplants in halves till soft and pearled; peel and process with garlic, salt, pepper, paprika and lemon juice; add olive oil and keep blending to an unctuous cream.

lamb
and mango skewers

■□□ | Cooking time: 10 minutes - Preparation time: 30 minutes

ingredients

> 1 kg/2 lb lean lamb, trimmed of visible fat and cut into 2 cm/3/4 in cubes
> 3 mangoes, cut into 2 cm/3/4 in cubes

hoisin-soy marinade

> 1 tablespoon finely grated fresh ginger
> 3/4 cup/185 ml/6 fl oz hoisin sauce
> 1/4 cup/60 ml/2 fl oz reduced-salt soy sauce
> 1/4 cup/60 ml/2 fl oz rice wine vinegar
> 1/4 cup/60 ml/2 fl oz vegetable oil

method

1. Use 24 wooden skewers (a). Soak in cold water for at least 30 minutes before threading meat.
2. To make marinade, place ginger, hoisin and soy sauces, vinegar and oil in a bowl and mix to combine. Add lamb, toss to coat (b), cover and marinate in the refrigerator for at least 4 hours.
3. Thread lamb and mango cubes, alternately, onto oiled skewers (c). Cook on a preheated hot barbecue for 3-4 minutes each side or until tender.

....
Serves 8

tip from the chef
These tasty skewers can be made with pineapple instead of mango.

a

b

c

two-toppings
crostini

■□□ | Cooking time: 12 minutes - Preparation time: 20 minutes

method

1. Brush bread slices with oil, place under a preheated hot grill and toast both sides until golden. Rub one side of toasts with cut side of garlic cloves.
2. For tomato and basil topping, top half the toast slices with some tomato, onion and basil, and grill for 1-2 minutes or until topping is warm.
3. For eggplant and feta topping, brush eggplant slices with oil and cook under preheated hot grill for 3-4 minutes each side or until lightly browned. Top remaining toasts with eggplant slices and sprinkle with feta cheese and black pepper to taste. Cook under a preheated hot grill for 1-2 minutes or until topping is warm.

Makes 16-20

ingredients

> **1 French bread stick, cut into 1 cm/^{1}/$_2$ in slices**
> **2 tablespoons olive oil**
> **2 cloves garlic, halved**

tomato and basil topping

> **2 tomatoes, sliced**
> **1 red onion, sliced**
> **2 tablespoons shredded basil leaves**

eggplant and feta topping

> **2 baby eggplant, sliced**
> **1 tablespoon olive oil**
> **125 g/4 oz feta cheese, crumbled**
> **freshly ground black pepper**

tip from the chef

Crostini, made from hot baguette slice toasts, can be topped with various pastes of cheese, olives or feta cheese with olive oil.

spicy
indian chicken

■■□ | Cooking time: 5 minutes - Preparation time: 35 minutes

ingredients

> **8 boneless chicken breast fillets, cut into 2.5 cm/1 in cubes**
> **1 cup/200 g/6 1/2 oz natural yogurt**
> **1 clove garlic, crushed**
> **1 teaspoon grated fresh ginger**
> **1/2 teaspoon garam masala**
> **1/4 teaspoon turmeric**
> **1/4 teaspoon ground cumin**
> **1 tablespoon chopped fresh coriander**
> **freshly ground black pepper**

cucumber coriander dip

> **1/2 cucumber, grated and drained**
> **1 tablespoon chopped fresh coriander**
> **1/2 cup/100 g/3 1/2 oz natural yogurt**
> **1/4 cup/60 ml/2 fl oz cream (double)**
> **freshly ground black pepper**

method

1. Place chicken, yogurt, garlic, ginger, garam masala, turmeric, cumin, coriander and black pepper to taste in a bowl and toss to combine. Cover and refrigerate for at least 4 hours or overnight.
2. Remove chicken from yogurt mixture and place in a single layer on a lightly greased baking tray. Cook under a preheated grill, for 5 minutes or until cooked. Spear 1 or 2 pieces of chicken onto wooden toothpicks.
3. To make dip, squeeze excess liquid from cucumber. Place cucumber, coriander, yogurt, cream and black pepper to taste in a bowl and mix to combine. Serve with chicken for dipping.

....

Serves 8

tip from the chef
Instead of cutting the chicken fillets into pieces, you can marinate them whole, then grill and serve with rice and salad for a tasty meal.

antipasto
skewers

■■□ | Cooking time: 5 minutes - Preparation time: 30 minutes

method

1. Place rosemary leaves, thyme leaves, vinegar and oil in a bowl and whisk to combine. Cut eggplant and zucchini into cubes. Add to vinegar mixture, then add tomatoes and red pepper. Toss to coat vegetables with marinade, cover and marinate for 30-60 minutes.

2. To make dipping sauce, place pesto, sour cream and black pepper to taste in a bowl and mix to combine.

3. Preheat barbecue to a high heat. Roll salami slices tightly. Drain vegetables and reserve marinade. Thread vegetables and salami rolls, alternately, onto small skewers. Cook skewers, brushing frequently with reserved marinade, on oiled barbecue grill for 1-2 minutes each side or until vegetables are tender. Serve skewers warm with dipping sauce.

....

Makes 12

ingredients

> **1 tablespoon fresh rosemary leaves**
> **1 tablespoon fresh thyme leaves**
> **1/4 cup/60 ml/2 fl oz balsamic vinegar**
> **2 tablespoons olive oil**
> **2 baby eggplant, halved lengthwise**
> **2 zucchini, halved lengthwise**
> **155 g/5 oz semi-dried tomatoes**
> **1 red pepper, diced**
> **250 g/8 oz sliced spicy salami**

creamy pesto dipping sauce

> **1/4 cup/60 ml/2 fl oz pesto**
> **1/2 cup/125 g/4 oz sour cream**
> **freshly ground black pepper**

tip from the chef

These skewers are best enjoyed before barbecues or outdoor lunches.

thai barbecue
fish cakes

■□□ | Cooking time: 3 minutes - Preparation time: 20 minutes

ingredients

> **375 g/12 oz boneless, fine fleshed, white fish fillets, chopped**
> **2 tablespoons red curry paste**
> **1 stalk fresh lemon grass, chopped or 1/2 teaspoon dried lemon grass, soaked in hot water until soft**
> **1 tablespoon chopped fresh coriander**
> **4 kaffir lime leaves, finely shredded**
> **1 egg white**
> **lime wedges**
> **sweet chili sauce**

method

1. Place fish, curry paste, lemon grass, coriander, lime leaves and egg white in a food processor and process until smooth.
2. Using wet or lightly oiled hands, take 1 tablespoon of mixture and roll into a ball, then flatten to form a disk. Repeat with remaining mixture. Place fish cakes on a tray lined with plastic food wrap and chill for 30 minutes or until firm.
3. Preheat barbecue to a high heat. Place fish cakes on oiled barbecue plate and cook for 1 minute each side or until cooked through. Serve with lime wedges and sweet chili sauce.

Makes 18

tip from the chef

These fish burgers go well with a fresh salad of bean sprouts, grated carrots and shredded cabbage.

tomato
salsa on bruschetta

■□□ | Cooking time: 8 minutes - Preparation time: 25 minutes

method

1. Preheat barbecue to a medium heat. To make the dressing, place garlic cloves on barbecue plate and cook for 1-2 minutes each side or until flesh is soft. Squeeze flesh from garlic cloves and mash. Place garlic, vinegar and oil in a screwtop jar and shake to combine.

2. To make salsa, place tomatoes and 2 tablespoons oil in a bowl and toss to coat. Place tomatoes, cut side down, on barbecue plate and cook for 1 minute each side. Place tomatoes, cheese, basil and black peppercorns to taste in a bowl, add dressing and toss to combine.

3. Lightly brush bread with oil, place on barbecue grill and toast for 1 minute each side. To serve, pile tomato salsa onto bread and serve immediately.

ingredients

> **12 slices crusty Italian bread**

grilled tomato salsa

> **500 g/1 lb cherry tomatoes, halved**
> **olive oil**
> **6 small bocconcini cheeses, chopped**
> **4 tablespoons torn fresh basil leaves**
> **crushed black peppercorns**

roasted garlic dressing

> **2 cloves garlic, unpeeled**
> **2 tablespoons balsamic vinegar**
> **1 tablespoon olive oil**

....
Makes 12

tip from the chef

Tomato, mozzarella and basil, with some drops of olive oil and a few turns of the pepper grinder, make up a unique and irreplaceable combination. As a salad, topping pizza crust, hot or cold, always delicious and welcome.

mediterranean
skewers

■■■ | Cooking time: 40 minutes - Preparation time: 1 hour

method

1. Place oregano and oil in a bowl. Add eggplant, zucchini, onions and peppers, toss to coat. Cover and stand 30-60 minutes.
2. To make focaccia, dissolve yeast with 1/2 cup lukewarm water and sugar. Combine flour and salt, place in a food processor and add yeast mixture. Process while gradually adding lukewarm water to form a dough. Cover with plastic food wrap and stand in a warm place until dough rises lightly. Roll out dough on a floured surface and place on an oiled baking tray. Sprinkle with grated cheese, coarse salt and oregano. Bake at 220°C/440°F/Gas 7 until golden and crisp. Cut diagonally into bars.
3. Preheat barbecue at high heat. Drain vegetables and reserve marinade. Thread vegetables and cheese, alternately, in skewers. Cook on grill, brushing frequently with marinade, 1-2 minutes each side or until vegetables are tender. Serve skewers with focaccia bars and garnish with fresh oregano.

ingredients

> 1 tablespoon chopped fresh oregano
> 8 tablespoons olive oil
> 2 eggplant, cut into thick slices
> 2 zucchini, cut into thick slices
> 2 onions, quartered
> 1 red pepper, cubed
> 1 green pepper, cubed
> 250 g/8 oz fontina cheese, cubed

oregano focaccia

> 15 g/1/2 oz fresh yeast
> 1 teaspoon sugar
> 250 g/8 oz flour
> 1 teaspoon salt
> 3 tablespoons olive oil
> 60 g/2 oz Parmesan cheese, grated
> 1 tablespoon coarse salt
> 1 tablespoon chopped fresh oregano
> fresh oregano to garnish

Serves 8

tip from the chef

These Mediterranean skewers can also be made with other vegetables, such as fennel, celery, cardoon. To vary and enhance aroma of focaccia, use chopped rosemary and garlic instead of oregano.

notes

Chef
express

sensational
salads

table of contents

introduction

There are so many varieties of salads as there
are countries, products, dressings and
condiments. The ideal dish for warm days,
the best option for a light meal, the customary
companion of all meats, the fresh starter
of family menus. And there is absolutely
no limit to the ingredients you can combine.

sensational salads
introduction

- Any product stored in the refrigerator, from chicken to beef, cheeses, eggs and bacon included, is good for making a tasty salad.
- Clean the vegetables thoroughly. Cut the most consistent ones into small pieces.
- To prevent fruit (apples, bananas, avocados) from darkening when cut, sprinkle with a dash of lemon juice.
- Combining green leaf salads with nuts (walnuts, hazelnuts, almonds) and cheeses results in a complete meal, since the vitamin content of vegetables is added to the calcium in cheese and the protein value of nuts, which also contain healthy unsaturated fat acids.
- A good salad is the ideal side dish for quiches, pizzas or any other food high in carbohydrates.

- Bean or alfalfa sprouts, add special flavors and textures.
- Smoked tofu (soybean cheese), sliced cheese and cottage cheese are savvy complements for different preparations.
- Flowers (honeysuckles, roses, calendulas, violets) add a fun note when preparing a salad for guests, provided the plants were not treated with pesticides or chemical fertilizers.
- All condiments are welcome as salad dressings.
- Seasonings can be prepared in advance, but should be incorporated at the time of serving, because oils and acids (vinegar, lemon) quickly degrade the texture of leaves and herbs.
- If stored in the refrigerator, salad should be taken out at least half an hour before serving. Room temperature enhances the combination of flavors.

Difficulty scale

■■☐☐ I Easy to do

■■■☐ I Requires attention

■■■■ I Requires experience

mexican salad

■□□ | Cooking time: 0 minutes - Preparation time: 5 minutes

ingredients

> **1 avocado, stoned, peeled and chopped**
> **1 tablespoon lime or lemon juice**
> **lettuce leaves of your choice**
> **2 tomatoes, cut into wedges**
> **1 green pepper, chopped**
> **315 g/10 oz canned red kidney beans, drained**
> **2 teaspoons chopped fresh coriander**
> **freshly ground black pepper**

method

1. Place avocado and lime or lemon juice in a small bowl and toss to coat.
2. Arrange lettuce leaves, tomatoes, green pepper, beans and avocado mixture attractively in two lunch boxes. Sprinkle with coriander and season to taste with black pepper. Cover and refrigerate until required.

Serves 2

tip from the chef
Tossing the avocado in lime or lemon juice helps prevent it from discoloring.

three
tomatoes salad

■□□ | Cooking time: 0 minutes - Preparation time: 15 minutes

method

1. Place egg (plum or Italian) tomatoes, cherry tomatoes, tomatoes, onion, vinegar, basil and black pepper to taste in a bowl and toss to combine. Set aside to stand for 30 minutes.
2. Line a large serving platter with lettuce leaves and top with tomato mixture.

Serves 6

ingredients

> **6 egg (plum or Italian) tomatoes, cut into wedges**
> **250 g/8 oz cherry tomatoes, halved**
> **3 seasonal tomatoes, sliced**
> **1 red onion, chopped**
> **2 tablespoons red wine vinegar**
> **2 tablespoons chopped fresh basil**
> **freshly ground black pepper**
> **assorted lettuce leaves**

tip from the chef

This salad can be made using any combination of tomatoes – so check the market and use what is in season and available.

salad
with hot dressing

■□□ | Cooking time: 0 minutes - Preparation time: 25 minutes

ingredients

> **375 g/12 oz canned sweet corn kernels, drained**
> **375 g/12 oz canned red kidney beans, rinsed and drained**
> **90 g/3 oz green beans, blanched and cut into 5 cm/2 in pieces**
> **1 large red pepper, diced**
> **1 large green pepper, diced**
> **3 tomatoes, chopped**
> **2 avocados, chopped**

chili and herb dressing

> **1 red onion, chopped**
> **3 small fresh green chilies, finely chopped**
> **2 cloves garlic, crushed**
> **3 tablespoons chopped fresh coriander**
> **2 teaspoons ground cumin**
> **1/3 cup/90 ml/3 fl oz balsamic vinegar**
> **1/4 cup/60 ml/2 fl oz olive oil**

method

1. Place sweet corn, red kidney and green beans, red and green peppers, tomatoes and avocados in a salad bowl and toss to combine.
2. To make dressing, place onion, chilies, garlic, coriander, cumin, vinegar and oil in a bowl and whisk to combine.
3. Drizzle dressing over salad and toss to combine. Cover and refrigerate for 1 hour before serving.

....
Serves 6

tip from the chef

To blanch green beans, bring a large saucepan of water to the boil, add beans and cook until they are bright green. Remove immediately and refresh under cold running water. For a delicious light meal serve this salad on fried tortillas or wrapped in pitta bread.

waldorf salad

■□□ | Cooking time: 0 minutes - Preparation time: 20 minutes

method

1. Place green apples, red apple, celery, walnuts and parsley in a bowl and toss to combine.
2. Place sour cream, mayonnaise and black pepper to taste in a small bowl and mix to combine. Add mayonnaise mixture to apple mixture and toss to combine. Cover and chill.

Serves 6

ingredients

> 2 large green eating apples, cored and diced
> 1 large red eating apple, cored and diced
> 3 stalks celery, diced
> 60 g/2 oz walnut pieces
> 1 tablespoon chopped fresh parsley
> 1/4 cup/60 g/2 oz sour cream
> 1/4 cup/60 ml/2 fl oz mayonnaise
> freshly ground black pepper

tip from the chef

This salad can be made in advance, but if making more than 2 hours ahead toss apples in 1 tablespoon lemon juice to prevent them from browning.

basil, orange and peach salad

■■■□ | Cooking time: 0 minutes - Preparation time: 30 minutes

ingredients

> **1 bunch fresh basil**
> **6 navel oranges, peeled and segmented**
> **3 orange peaches, peeled and sliced**
> **1 red onion, sliced**
> **2 tablespoons red wine vinegar**
> **1 garlic clove, crushed**
> **2 tablespoons unsweetened apple juice**
> **2 tablespoons safflower oil**

method

1. Wash and dry basil leaves, arrange on a serving plate.
2. In a small bowl combine orange segments, peach slices and onion.
3. Mix together vinegar, garlic, apple juice and oil until well combined and pour over oranges, peaches and onion.
4. Toss well, and arrange on top of bed of basil. Serve immediately.

Serves 6

tip from the chef

This salad, like all the ones made of only herbs and fruit, is both nourishing and adequate not to put on weight. If you want to be in shape, replace a main dish by a salad, rich in vitamins and minerals and low in calories.

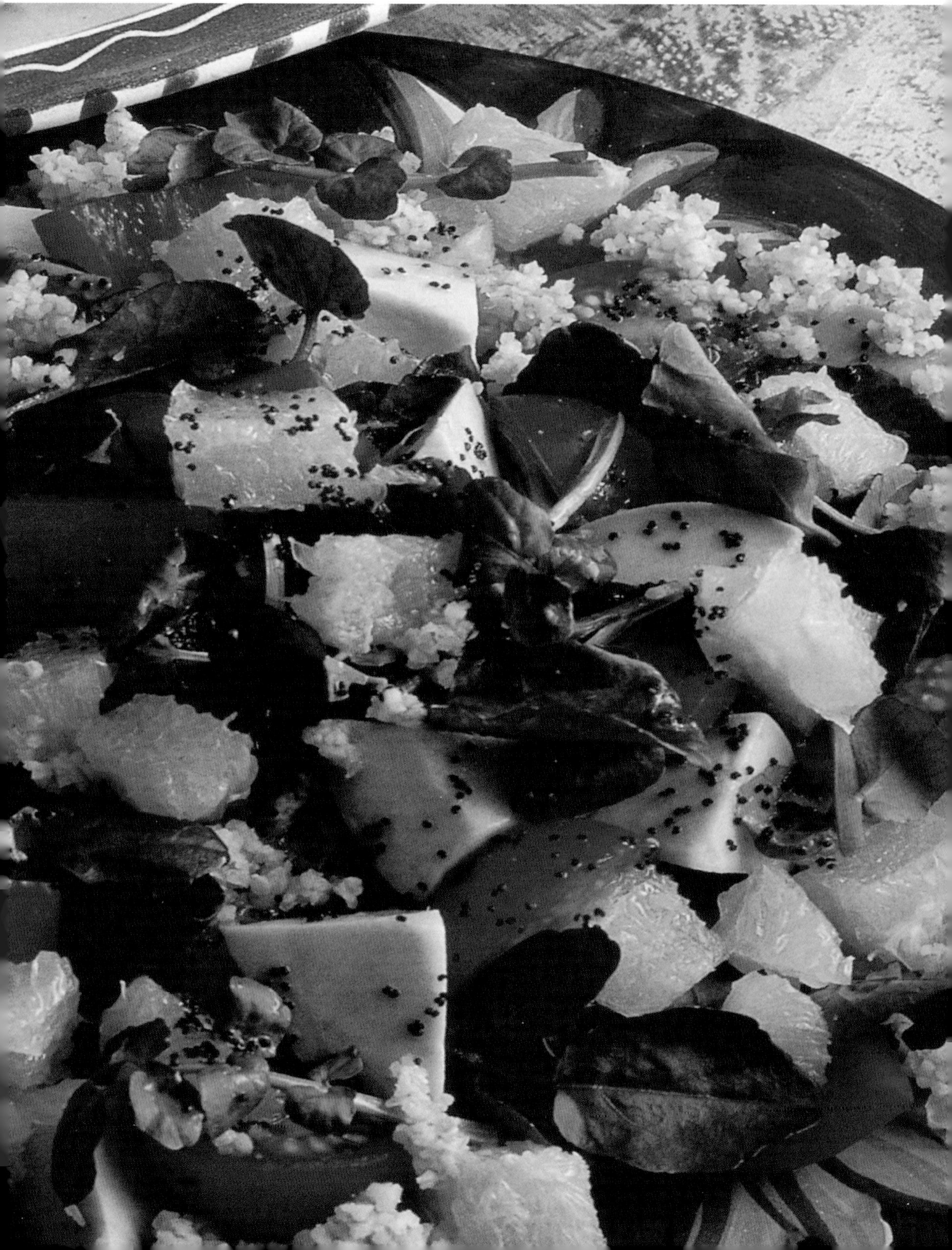

watercress
and orange salad

▪▪☐ | Cooking time: 0 minutes - Preparation time: 25 minutes

method

1. Place burghul in a bowl, cover with boiling water and allow to stand for 10-15 minutes or until soft. Drain.
2. Place burghul, watercress, avocado, oranges, tomatoes and red pepper in a salad bowl.
3. To make dressing, place orange juice, poppy seeds and vinegar in a screw-top jar and shake well to combine. Spoon dressing over salad and toss to combine. Cover and chill until required.

Serves 4

ingredients

> 1 cup/185 g/6 oz burghul
> 2 cups/500 ml/16 fl oz boiling water
> 1 bunch/250 g/8 oz watercress, broken into sprigs
> 1 avocado, stoned, peeled and chopped
> 2 oranges, white pith removed, flesh chopped
> 250 g/8 oz cherry tomatoes, halved
> 1 red pepper, diced

orange dressing

> 1/2 cup/125 ml/4 fl oz orange juice
> 1 tablespoon poppy seeds
> 2 tablespoons red wine vinegar

tip from the chef

The combination of orange and avocado is always great. Watercress contributes the necessary amount of iron. If a more substantial salad is wanted, diced feta cheese can be added.

orange and spinach salad

■ ■ □ | Cooking time: 0 minutes - Preparation time: 30 minutes

ingredients

> **6 oranges, peeled and all white pith removed, sliced crosswise**
> **2 red onions, sliced**
> **90 g/3 oz toasted almonds, chopped**
> **2 medium fresh red chilies, chopped**
> **1/2 bunch fresh coriander**
> **4 tablespoons fresh mint leaves**
> **1/4 bunch/125 g/4 oz spinach, leaves shredded**

method

1. Place oranges, onions, almonds, chilies, coriander leaves and mint in a bowl, toss to combine and stand for 30 minutes. Line a serving platter with spinach, then pile salad on top.

....
Serves 6

tip from the chef

Garnish with extra red onion and serve with grilled meats or chicken.

spiral pasta salad

■■■□ | Cooking time: 10 minutes - Preparation time: 30 minutes

method

1. Cook pasta in boiling water in a large saucepan following packet directions. Drain, rinse under cold running water and set aside to cool completely.

2. Place pasta, sun-dried tomatoes, artichokes, sun-dried or roasted peppers, olives, basil, Parmesan cheese, oil and vinegar in a bowl and toss to combine. Cover and refrigerate for 2 hours or until ready to serve.

Serves 4

ingredients

> **500 g/1 lb spiral pasta**
> **100 g/3¹/₂ oz sun-dried tomatoes, thinly sliced**
> **100 g/3¹/₂ oz marinated artichoke hearts, chopped**
> **75 g/2¹/₂ oz sun-dried or roasted peppers, chopped**
> **125 g/4 oz marinated black olives**
> **12 small fresh basil leaves**
> **60 g/2 oz Parmesan cheese shavings**
> **1 tablespoon olive oil**
> **3 tablespoons balsamic or red wine vinegar**

tip from the chef

A wonderful salad that combines all the best flavors of Italy. It is delicious served with crusty bread and baked ricotta cheese. If you can, make it a day in advance so that the flavors have time to develop.

minestrone salad

■■■□ I Cooking time: 10 minutes - Preparation time: 40 minutes

ingredients

- > **250 g/8 oz pasta shells**
- > **440 g/14 oz canned chickpeas, rinsed and drained**
- > **2 carrots, diced**
- > **2 zucchini, diced**
- > **2 stalks celery, diced**
- > **1 red pepper, diced**
- > **155 g/5 oz green beans, blanched**
- > **3 plum (egg or Italian) tomatoes, cut into wedges**
- > **250 g/8 oz mixed lettuce leaves**

pesto dressing

- > **125 g/4 oz ready-made pesto**
- > **1/2 cup/100 g/3 1/2 oz natural yogurt**
- > **2 tablespoons mayonnaise**

method

1. Cook pasta in boiling water in a large saucepan following packet directions. Drain, rinse under cold running water and set aside to cool completely.
2. Place chickpeas, carrots, zucchini, celery, red pepper, beans, tomatoes and pasta in a bowl and toss to combine.
3. Arrange lettuce on a serving platter and top with pasta mixture.
4. To make dressing, place pesto, yogurt and mayonnaise in a bowl and mix to combine. Drizzle over salad and serve.

Serves 4

tip from the chef

This dish makes the most of all the flavors ordinarily found in minestrone soup and serves them up as a salad! If plum (egg or Italian) tomatoes are not available, use ordinary tomatoes.

chili
broad bean salad

■ ■ □ | Cooking time: 25 minutes - Preparation time: 35 minutes

method

1. Cook pasta in boiling water in a large saucepan, following packet directions. Drain, rinse under cold running water, then drain again and set aside to cool completely.
2. Heat oil in a large frying pan and cook broad beans and chili paste over a medium heat for 3 minutes. Stir in stock, bring to a simmer, cover and cook for 10 minutes. Drain off any remaining liquid and set aside to cool.
3. To make dressing, place oil, vinegar, garlic and black pepper to taste in a screw-top jar. Shake well to combine.
4. Place pasta, broad bean mixture, radishes, parsley and Parmesan cheese in a salad bowl. Pour dressing over and toss to combine.

Serves 4

ingredients

> 375 g/12 oz small shell pasta
> 1 tablespoon vegetable oil
> 250 g/8 oz shelled or frozen broad beans
> 1 teaspoon chili paste (sambal oelek)
> 1¹/₂ cups/375 ml/ 12 fl oz chicken stock
> 6 radishes, thinly sliced
> 2 tablespoons chopped fresh parsley
> 30 g/1 oz grated fresh Parmesan cheese

garlic dressing

> ¹/₄ cup/60 ml/2 fl oz olive oil
> 1 tablespoon cider vinegar
> 1 clove garlic, crushed
> freshly ground black pepper

tip from the chef

Short pasta is the ideal complement for summer salads. It contributes slow assimilation hidrocarbons, allowing outdoor activities and sports after the meal.

thai squid salad

■■■□ | Cooking time: 5 minutes - Preparation time: 40 minutes

ingredients

> **3 squid tubes, cleaned**
> **185 g/6 oz green beans, sliced lengthwise**
> **2 tomatoes, cut into wedges**
> **1 small green pawpaw, peeled, seeded and shredded**
> **4 spring onions, sliced**
> **30 g/1 oz fresh mint leaves**
> **30 g/1 oz fresh coriander leaves**
> **1 fresh red chili, chopped**

lime dressing

> **2 teaspoons brown sugar**
> **3 tablespoons lime juice**
> **1 tablespoon fish sauce**

method

1. Using a sharp knife, make a single cut down the length of each squid tube (a) and open out. Cut parallel lines down the length of the squid, taking care not to cut right the way through the flesh. Make more cuts in the opposite direction (b) to form a diamond pattern.
2. Heat a nonstick char-grill or frying pan over a high heat, add squid and cook for 1-2 minutes each side (c) or until tender. Remove from pan and cut into thin strips.
3. Place squid, beans, tomatoes, pawpaw, spring onions, mint, coriander and chili in a serving bowl.
4. To make dressing, place sugar, lime juice and fish sauce in a screw-top jar and shake well. Drizzle over salad and toss to combine. Cover and stand for 20 minutes before serving.

Serves 4

tip from the chef

It is best to serve the dressings and sauces separately, so guests can help themselves.

a

b

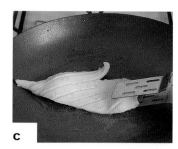

c

niçoise salad

■■□ | Cooking time: 0 minutes - Preparation time: 50 minutes

method

1. To make salad, place tuna, artichokes, if using, cheese, eggs, potatoes, tomatoes, onion, beans and olives in a large bowl and toss to combine.
2. To make dressing, place oil, vinegar, garlic, mustard and black pepper to taste in a screw-top jar and shake well to combine. Spoon dressing over salad and toss lightly.
3. Line a large serving platter with lettuce leaves and top with salad.

....

Serves 6

ingredients

> **lettuce leaves of choice**

tuna salad
> **440 g/14 oz canned tuna, drained and flaked**
> **125 g/4 oz canned artichoke hearts, drained and sliced (optional)**
> **125 g/4 oz tasty cheese (mature Cheddar), cubed**
> **4 hard-boiled eggs, sliced**
> **2 potatoes, cooked and sliced**
> **2 tomatoes, sliced**
> **1 onion, sliced**
> **250 g/8 oz green beans, cooked**
> **45 g/1 1/2 oz stuffed olives, sliced**

niçoise dressing
> **1/4 cup/60 ml/2 fl oz olive oil**
> **2 tablespoons vinegar**
> **1 clove garlic, crushed**
> **1/2 teaspoon Dijon mustard**
> **freshly ground black pepper**

tip from the chef

For a complete meal, serve with crusty fresh or toasted French bread. A few anchovies and shavings of Parmesan cheese are great additions to this dish. Always buy the form of the product that best fits your menu. Less expensive shredded or flaked tuna is the perfect choice for a salad such as this – it's lower priced because of appearance, not quality. Feta cheese makes a delicious and more gourmet alternative to tasty cheese (mature Cheddar).

asparagus and salmon salad

■□□ | Cooking time: 7 minutes - Preparation time: 20 minutes

ingredients

> **750 g/1¹/2 lb asparagus spears, trimmed**
> **lettuce leaves of your choice**
> **500 g/1 lb smoked salmon slices**
> **freshly ground black pepper**

lemon yogurt sauce

> **1 cup/200 g/6¹/2 oz natural yogurt**
> **1 tablespoon finely grated lemon rind**
> **1 tablespoon lemon juice**
> **1 tablespoon chopped fresh dill**
> **1 teaspoon ground cumin**

method

1. Boil, steam or microwave asparagus until tender. Drain, refresh under cold running water, drain again and chill. Arrange lettuce leaves, asparagus and salmon on serving plates.
2. To make sauce, place yogurt, lemon rind, lemon juice, dill and cumin in a small bowl and mix to combine.
3. Spoon sauce over salad. Sprinkle with black pepper, cover and chill until required.

....
Serves 6

tip from the chef

If fresh asparagus is unavailable, green beans or snow peas are good alternatives for this recipe.

grilled prawn salad

■■□ | Cooking time: 2 minutes - Preparation time: 30 minutes

method

1. Place prawns, chili, soy sauce and honey (a) in a bowl, toss to combine and marinate for 5 minutes.
2. Arrange chicory, radicchio, mangoes, mint and coriander on serving plates. Combine sugar and lime juice in a small bowl (b) and drizzle over salad.
3. Heat a nonstick frying pan over a high heat, add prawns (c) and stir-fry for 2 minutes or until cooked. Place prawns on top of salad, spoon over pan juices and serve immediately.

....

Serves 4

ingredients

> 16 uncooked prawns, shelled and deveined, tails left intact
> 1 fresh green chili, seeded and shredded
> 1/4 cup/60 ml/2 fl oz light soy sauce
> 1 tablespoon honey
> 1 chicory, leaves separated
> 1 radicchio, leaves separated
> 2 green (unripe) mangoes, thinly sliced
> 4 tablespoons fresh mint leaves
> 3 tablespoons fresh coriander leaves
> 1 tablespoon brown sugar
> 2 tablespoons lime juice

tip from the chef

This prawn salad must be prepared and served at once.

a

b

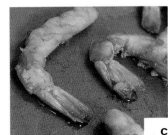

c

chicken
caesar salad

■■□ | Cooking time: 25 minutes - Preparation time: 35 minutes

ingredients

> **2 boneless chicken breast fillets**
> **4 rashers bacon**
> **1 cos lettuce, leaves separated**
> **250 g/8 oz cherry tomatoes, halved**
> **125 g/4 oz Parmesan cheese shavings**

crispy croûtons

> **250 g/8 oz bread cubes**
> **2 tablespoons olive oil**

creamy mustard dressing

> **$^1/_2$ cup/125 g/4 oz sour cream**
> **$^1/_2$ cup/125 ml/4 fl oz mayonnaise**
> **2 tablespoons wholegrain mustard**
> **3 anchovy fillets, chopped**
> **$^1/_4$ cup/60 ml/2 fl oz water**

method

1. Preheat barbecue to a medium heat.
2. To make croutons, place bread cubes in a baking dish, drizzle with oil and toss to coat. Bake for 15 minutes or until bread is crisp and golden. Cool.
3. Place chicken and bacon on oiled barbecue and cook for 2-3 minutes each side or until chicken is tender and bacon is crisp. Cool, then cut chicken into slices and chop bacon.
4. Arrange lettuce leaves, tomatoes, chicken and bacon in a bowl.
5. To make dressing, place sour cream, mayonnaise, mustard, anchovies and water in a food processor or blender and process until smooth. Just prior to serving, drizzle dressing over salad, then scatter with croûtons and Parmesan cheese shavings.

Serves 8

tip from the chef

To make the bread cubes for the croûtons, take an unsliced loaf of stale bread and cut off all the crusts to make an evenly shaped rectangular loaf. Cut bread loaf into 5 mm/$^1/_4$ in thick slices. Cut each bread slice into 5 mm/$^1/_4$ in thick strips, then cut in the opposite direction at 5 mm/$^1/_4$ in intervals to make 5 mm/$^1/_4$ in square bread cubes. Leftover croûtons will keep in an airtight container for several weeks.

new mexico
chicken salad

■□□ | Cooking time: 0 minutes - Preparation time: 20 minutes

method

1. Arrange rocket, flowers and radicchio attractively on serving plates. Top with grapefruit and chicken.
2. To make dressing, place pine nuts, bay leaves, chilies, sugar, vinegar and oil in a bowl and whisk to combine. Just prior to serving, drizzle dressing over salad.

Serves 4

ingredients

> 1 bunch young rocket
> edible flowers of your choice
> 6 radicchio leaves, shredded
> 1 grapefruit, peeled, all white pith removed, segmented
> 2 smoked chicken breasts, sliced

pine nut and chili dressing

> 4 tablespoons pine nuts, toasted
> 6 bay leaves
> 2 fresh red chilies, finely chopped
> 2 tablespoons sugar
> 1/3 cup/90 ml/3 fl oz red wine vinegar
> 1/4 cup/60 ml/2 fl oz olive oil

tip from the chef

Edible flowers you might like to choose from include nasturtiums, scented geraniums, roses, marigolds, violets, zucchini flowers and the flowers of most herbs such as chives, rocket, borage, dill, rosemary, lavender and basil. Look out for mixed packs of edible flowers in greengrocers and specialty food shops.

spinach
and bacon salad

■□□ | Cooking time: 7 minutes - Preparation time: 20 minutes

ingredients

> **1 tablespoon olive oil**
> **4 rashers bacon, chopped**
> **90 g/3 oz slivered almonds**
> **1 bunch/500 g/1 lb spinach, roughly chopped**

blue cheese dressing

> **60 g/2 oz blue cheese, crumbled**
> **1 tablespoon mayonnaise**
> **1 tablespoon sour cream**
> **1/4 cup/60 ml/2 fl oz cream (double)**

method

1. Heat oil in a large frying pan, add bacon and cook over a medium heat for 3-4 minutes or until bacon is crispy. Add almonds and cook, stirring, for 3 minutes longer or until almonds are golden.
2. Arrange spinach on a large serving platter, top with bacon, almonds and any pan juices and toss to combine.
3. To make dressing, place cheese, mayonnaise, sour cream and cream in a bowl and mix to combine. Drizzle dressing over salad and serve immediately.

Serves 4

tip from the chef

The hot bacon mixture will wilt the spinach leaves slightly. The secret to making warm salads such as this one is to make and serve them immediately. For a complete meal, serve with crusty bread or rolls.

green salad
in creamy dressing

| | Cooking time: 5 minutes - Preparation time: 30 minutes

method

1. Cook bacon in a frying pan over a medium heat for 4-5 minutes or until crisp. Remove bacon from pan and drain on absorbent kitchen paper until cool.
2. Arrange lettuces, tomatoes, carrots, celery, snow peas and bacon on a serving platter or in a large salad bowl.
3. To make dressing, place mayonnaise, sour cream, lemon juice and black pepper to taste in a bowl and mix to combine. Drizzle dressing over salad, cover and chill until required.

Serves 10

ingredients

> **6 rashers bacon, chopped**
> **2 lettuces of your choice, leaves separated and torn into pieces**
> **250 g/8 oz cherry tomatoes, halved**
> **2 carrots, cut into strips**
> **2 sticks celery, cut into strips**
> **125 g/4 oz snow peas**

creamy dressing

> **1/2 cup/125 g/4 oz mayonnaise**
> **1/2 cup/125 g/4 oz sour cream**
> **1 tablespoon lemon juice**
> **freshly ground black pepper**

tip from the chef

For best results, bacon must be cooked just before mixing it with vegetables, so it remains crispy until serving time.

cellophane
noodle salad

■□□ I Cooking time: 6 minutes - Preparation time: 30 minutes

ingredients

> **155 g/5 oz cellophane noodles**
> **2 teaspoons sesame oil**
> **2 cloves garlic, crushed**
> **1 tablespoon finely grated fresh ginger**
> **4 rashers bacon, chopped**
> **500 g/1 lb pork mince**
> **15 g/¹/₂ oz mint leaves**
> **15 g/¹/₂ oz coriander leaves**
> **8 lettuce leaves**
> **5 red or golden shallots, chopped**
> **1 fresh red chili, sliced**
> **2 tablespoons lemon juice**
> **1 tablespoon light soy sauce**

method

1. Place noodles in a bowl and pour over boiling water to cover. Stand for 10 minutes, then drain well.
2. Heat oil in a frying pan over a high heat, add garlic and ginger and stir-fry for 1 minute. Add bacon and pork and stir-fry for 5 minutes or until pork is browned and cooked through.
3. Arrange mint, coriander, lettuce, shallots, chili and noodles on a serving platter. Top with pork mixture, then drizzle with lemon juice and soy sauce.

Serves 4

tip from the chef

Cellophane noodles, also known as glass noodles, bean thread noodles or vermicelli, are made from mung bean flour and are either very thin vermicelli-style noodles or flatter fettuccine-style noodles. In the dried state they are very tough and difficult to break. For ease of use it is better to buy a brand which packages them as bundles.

tofu salad

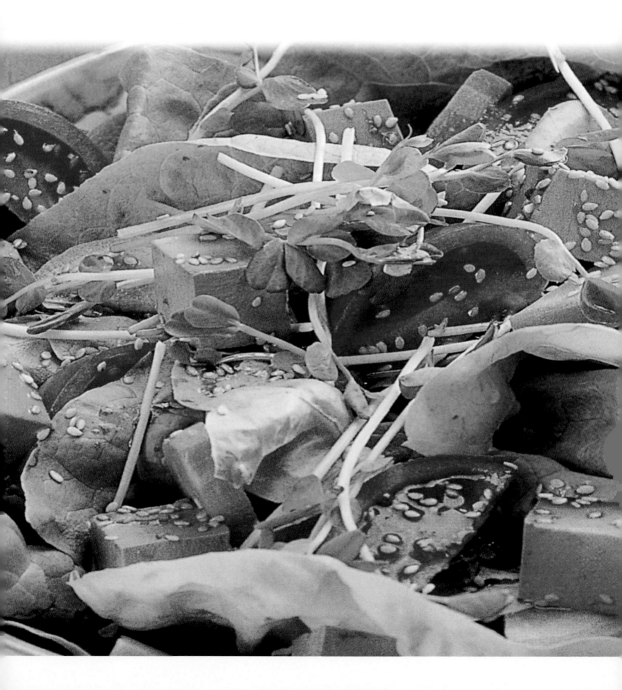

■■□□ | Cooking time: 0 minutes - Preparation time: 25 minutes

method

1. Place soy sauce, oil, ginger, lemon juice and wine in a small bowl. Add tofu and toss to coat. Cover and set aside to marinate for 10-15 minutes.
2. Place lettuce, tomatoes, snow pea sprouts or watercress and carrots in a bowl. Drain tofu and reserve marinade. Add tofu to salad, toss to combine and sprinkle with sesame seeds. Just prior to serving, drizzle with reserved marinade.

Serves 4

ingredients

> 4 tablespoons soy sauce
> 2 teaspoons vegetable oil
> 1/2 teaspoon finely chopped fresh ginger
> 1 tablespoon lemon juice
> 2 teaspoons dry white wine
> 500 g/1 lb tofu, cut into cubes
> 1 lettuce, leaves separated
> 2 tomatoes, cut into wedges
> 60 g/2 oz snow pea sprouts or watercress
> 2 carrots, sliced
> 1 tablespoon sesame seeds, toasted

tip from the chef

An easy summer meal, this salad requires only wholegrain or rye bread to make it a complete meal.

bean salad

■□□ | Cooking time: 0 minutes - Preparation time: 25 minutes

ingredients

> **1 cup canned red kidney beans, rinsed and drained**
> **1 cup canned chickpeas, rinsed and drained**
> **1 cup canned pinto beans, rinsed and drained**
> **1 cup green beans, blanched**
> **2 zucchini, blanched and sliced into strips**
> **1 carrot, blanched and sliced into strips**
> **1/2 cup water-chestnuts, drained**
> **2 pimentos, sliced into strips**
> **2 tablespoons chopped fresh parsley**
> **1 tablespoon chopped fresh basil**
> **1/2 cup Italian dressing**

method

1. Combine red kidney beans, chickpeas, pinto beans, green beans, zucchini, carrot, chestnuts, pimentos, parsley, basil and Italian dressing in a large bowl.
2. Toss well, cover and refrigerate 4 to 6 hours. Toss again before serving; serve chilled.

....
Serves 6

tip from the chef

As an alternative, this salad can be seasoned with a mixture of yogurt and Dijon mustard in place of Italian dressing.

mushroom
and pimento salad

■□□ | Cooking time: 0 minutes - Preparation time: 30 minutes

method

1. In a medium bowl, mix together lemon juice, red vinegar, white vinegar, garlic, basil, parsley and oil, until well combined.
2. Stir in the pimentos and mushrooms, cover and chill for 3 hours. Serve chilled as a side dish.

....
Serves 4

ingredients

> **2 tablespoons lemon juice**
> **2 tablespoons red wine vinegar**
> **2 tablespoons white wine vinegar**
> **2 cloves garlic, crushed**
> **1 tablespoon chopped fresh basil**
> **1 tablespoon chopped fresh parsley**
> **2 tablespoons safflower oil**
> **8 pimentos, sliced into strips**
> **1 cup mushrooms, sliced**

tip from the chef

Excellent as an accompaniment to barbecued meats.

zucchini salad

■□□ | Cooking time: 0 minutes - Preparation time: 15 minutes

method

1. Place zucchini and onion in a bowl.
2. To make dressing, place dill, parsley, garlic, vinegar, oil, lemon juice and black pepper to taste in bowl and whisk to combine. Pour over zucchini mixture and toss. Cover and chill for at least 1 hour before serving.

....

Serves 8

ingredients

> **6 zucchini, thinly sliced lengthwise**
> **1 onion, sliced**

fresh herb dressing

> **2 tablespoons chopped fresh dill**
> **1 tablespoon chopped fresh parsley**
> **1 clove garlic, crushed**
> **¼ cup/60 ml/2 fl oz white vinegar**
> **2 tablespoons olive oil**
> **1 tablespoon lemon juice**
> **freshly ground black pepper**

tip from the chef

This salad can be completed with steamed potatoes, and dressed with tarragon mayonnaise.

balsamic
tomato salad

■□□ | Cooking time: 0 minutes - Preparation time: 10 minutes

method

1. Place tomatoes, cheese, onion and basil in a bowl and toss to combine.
2. To make dressing, place sugar, vinegar and black pepper to taste in a screw-top jar and shake well to combine. Pour dressing over tomato mixture and toss to combine. Cover and marinate, at room temperature, for 20 minutes before serving.

....

Serves 4

ingredients

> **4 tomatoes, thickly sliced**
> **125 g/4 oz feta cheese, chopped**
> **1/2 red onion, sliced**
> **3 tablespoons fresh basil leaves**

balsamic dressing

> **1 tablespoon brown sugar**
> **1/4 cup/60 ml/2 fl oz balsamic vinegar**
> **freshly ground black pepper**

tip from the chef

If stronger flavors are preferred, use brie or camembert instead of feta cheese. As a dressing, use a good olive oil seasoned with garlic and fresh thyme leaves.

warm
potato salad

■□□ | Cooking time: 7 minutes - Preparation time: 5 minutes

ingredients

> **500 g/1 lb baby new potatoes**

mustard dressing
> **2 tablespoons wholegrain mustard**
> **2 tablespoons chopped fresh parsley**
> **2 teaspoons chopped capers**
> **1 clove garlic, crushed**
> **1 tablespoon lemon juice**
> **freshly ground black pepper**

method

1. Cook potatoes in boiling water until just tender. Drain well and place in a heatproof bowl.
2. To make dressing, place mustard, parsley, capers, garlic, lemon juice and black pepper to taste in a bowl and mix to combine. Spoon dressing over hot potatoes and toss to combine. Serve immediately.

....
Serves 4

tip from the chef
Iced water or mineral water makes a refreshing and light drink to serve with salads. For added appeal serve with a slice of lemon, lime or orange.

hot potato salad

■□□ | Cooking time: 16 minutes - Preparation time: 20 minutes

method

1. Using a sharp knife, score around the circumference of each potato.
2. Place potatoes evenly around edge of microwave turntable and cook on High (100%) for
   5 minutes, turn over and cook for
   3-5 minutes longer or until potatoes are cooked. Set aside until cool enough to handle, then remove skin and cut potatoes into 1 cm/1/2 in cubes.
3. Place onion and bacon in a microwavable bowl, cover and cook on High (100%) for 3 minutes, stir, then cook for 2 minutes longer.
4. Stir in cornflour, stock and vinegar, cover and cook for 4 minutes. Add mustard, cream and potatoes and mix gently to combine. Cover and cook on Medium (50%) for 2 minutes or until hot. Season to taste with black pepper and sprinkle with chives. Serve warm.

ingredients

> 4 red-skinned potatoes, about 750 g/11/2 lb
> 1 onion, diced
> 2 rashers bacon, chopped
> 2 tablespoons cornflour
> 1 cup/250 ml/8 fl oz vegetable stock
> 1/4 cup/60 ml/2 fl oz cider or tarragon vinegar
> 1 tablespoon wholegrain mustard
> 1/3 cup/90 ml/3 fl oz cream (double)
> freshly ground black pepper
> snipped fresh chives

....
Serves 6

tip from the chef

This is a good hot dish to serve at a salad buffet or barbecue. Flat oval-shaped potatoes seem to cook the most evenly in the microwave.

roasted
vegetable salad

■■□ I Cooking time: 35 minutes - Preparation time: 30 minutes

ingredients

> **3 bulbs fennel, cut into wedges**
> **2 sweet potatoes, peeled and chopped**
> **12 shallots, peeled**
> **olive oil spray**
> **1 teaspoon cumin seeds**
> **315 g/10 oz green beans, blanched**
> **185 g/6 oz rocket leaves**
> **155 g/5 oz feta cheese, chopped**
> **2-3 tablespoons balsamic vinegar**
> **freshly ground black pepper**

method

1. Place fennel, sweet potatoes and shallots in a nonstick baking dish (a) and spray with olive oil. Sprinkle with cumin seeds (b) and bake at 180°C/350°F/Gas 4 for 30-35 minutes or until vegetables are soft and golden. Set aside to cool for 10-15 minutes or until vegetables are warm.

2. Place vegetables in a serving bowl, add beans, rocket, cheese, vinegar and black pepper to taste and toss.

··········
Serves 4

tip from the chef
The shallots used in this recipe are the French échalote. If unavailable, red or yellow shallots or pickling onions can be used instead.

a

b

salad
of roast tomatoes

■□□ | Cooking time: 30 minutes - Preparation time: 15 minutes

method

1. Place tomatoes and garlic on a baking tray (a), sprinkle with black pepper to taste and oil (b) and bake at 180°C/350°F/Gas 4 for 30 minutes or until tomatoes are soft and golden (c). Set aside to cool completely.

2. Arrange lettuce leaves, feta cheese, pepper, tomatoes and garlic attractively on serving plates.

3. To make dressing, place vinegar, tomato purée, Tabasco and black pepper to taste in a screw-top jar and shake well to combine. Drizzle dressing over salad and serve immediately.

....

Serves 4

ingredients

> 6 plum (egg or Italian) tomatoes, halved
> 8 cloves garlic, peeled
> freshly ground black pepper
> 2 tablespoons olive oil
> 315 g/10 oz assorted lettuce leaves
> 185 g/6 oz feta cheese, crumbled
> 1 yellow or red pepper, sliced

tangy dressing

> 3 tablespoons balsamic or red wine vinegar
> 3 tablespoons tomato purée
> 3 drops Tabasco sauce

tip from the chef

The sweet rich flavor of roast tomatoes is a perfect partner for the creamy piquant feta cheese in this salad.

a

b

c

warm
vegetable salad

■ ■ □ | Cooking time: 11 minutes - Preparation time: 30 minutes

method

1. To make vinaigrette, place olive oil, vinegar, thyme, sugar and black pepper to taste in a screw-top jar and shake well to combine. Set aside.
2. Heat 2 teaspoons vegetable oil in a wok over a high heat, add hazelnuts (a) and stir-fry for 3 minutes. Set aside. Heat remaining oil in wok, add onions (b) and stir-fry for 3 minutes or until golden.
3. Add carrots, zucchini, green beans (c), mushrooms, green and red peppers, spring onions and asparagus and stir-fry for 5 minutes.
4. Mix vegetables and hazelnuts, add vinaigrette and toss to combine. Serve warm.

....
Serves 4

ingredients

> 1 tablespoon vegetable oil
> 125 g/4 oz blanched hazelnuts
> 2 onions, chopped
> 2 carrots, sliced
> 2 zucchini, chopped
> 155 g/5 oz green beans
> 4 field mushrooms, sliced
> 1 green pepper, sliced
> 1 red pepper, sliced
> 6 spring onions, chopped
> 250 g/8 oz asparagus, halved

thyme vinaigrette

> 1/3 cup/90 ml/3 fl oz olive oil
> 1/4 cup/60 ml/2 fl oz red wine vinegar
> 1 tablespoon chopped fresh thyme
> 1 teaspoon sugar
> freshly ground black pepper

tip from the chef

A heavy wok made of carbon steel will give better cooking results than a stainless steel or aluminum one.

a

b

c

notes

Chef
express
seafood
splendor

table of contents

introduction

Recent research shows that there are various reasons why we should eat seafood: it is low in fat and so low in calories; it contains many essential vitamins and minerals; it is a good source of protein; it contains Omega 3 fatty acids which have been shown to help prevent heart disease; and -best of all- it makes a delicious meal.

Nutritionists and health professionals now recommend that we eat seafood at least three times a week.

Buying fish and shellfish

- Fillets: Should be shiny and firm with a pleasant sea smell. Don't buy fillets that are dull, soft, discolored or 'ooze' water when touched.
- Whole fish: Should have a pleasant smell and a bright luster to the skin. Gills should be red and eyes bright and bulging. When touched, the flesh should be firm and springy. Dull-colored fish with sunken eyes should be avoided at all costs.
- Smoked fish: Should have a pleasant smoked smell and be dry. Avoid smoked fish that is 'sweaty' or slimy with a rancid smell.
- Lobster (cooked): Limbs should be intact, tails curled and eyes bright. The lobster should feel heavy in proportion to its size. Discoloration at the joints and missing or loose limbs indicate that the lobster is past its best.

- Mussels (live): Shells should be tightly closed. Open shells indicates that mussels are already dead.
- Oysters: Should be plump and shiny with a natural creamy color and clear liquid. They should have a pleasant sea smell and be free of shell particles.
- Prawns (cooked): Flesh should be firm and shells tight. Prawns should have a pleasant sea smell. Avoid limp-looking prawns with black loose heads or legs.
- Prawns (uncooked): Should have a firm body and pleasant sea smell, and show no sign of black.

Frozen seafood

- As with all food, if you plan to freeze seafood, it should be as fresh as possible.
- When buying frozen fish watch out for freezer burn; this appears as dry, white or brown patches and indicates that the fish has been wrapped incorrectly and has dehydrated.
- Frozen seafood is best cooked directly from frozen. Just allow a little extra cooking time. Cooking seafood this way ensures that it holds its shape and retains its flavor and texture better.

Difficulty scale

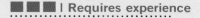

■ □ □ I Easy to do

■ ■ □ I Requires attention

■ ■ ■ I Requires experience

wine steamed mussels with orange segments

■ ■ □ □ | Cooking time: 15 minutes - Preparation time: 10 minutes

method

1. Heat oil in a large frying pan over medium heat. Add onions and garlic and cook for 2 minutes. Add oregano, orange strips and wine, cook for a further 2 minutes.
2. Increase heat, bring to the boil. Add mussels, cover and steam for 5 minutes. Transfer opened mussels to serving dish and discard any that do not open.
3. Stir parsley into mussel cooking liquid and bring to the boil. Stir in orange segments and pour sauce over mussels. Serve immediately.

Serves 2-3

ingredients

> **2 tablespoons oil**
> **1 onion, chopped**
> **3 cloves garlic, crushed**
> **2 tablespoons chopped oregano**
> **10 strips of orange rind**
> **1¹/₂ cups dry white wine**
> **800 g/1 lb 10 oz mussels, scrubbed and beards removed**
> **1 tablespoon chopped parsley**
> **1 orange, peeled and segmented**

tip from the chef

Mussels grow in clusters, attaching themselves by means of a "byssus" to rocks or other supports such as jetties or gravel beaches.

scallops provençal

◼☐☐ | Cooking time: 25 minutes - Preparation time: 15 minutes

ingredients

> **2 teaspoons olive oil**
> **1 onion, chopped**
> **2 cloves garlic, crushed**
> **440 g/14 oz canned tomatoes, undrained and mashed**
> **2 teaspoons finely chopped fresh thyme or 1/2 teaspoon dried thyme**
> **1/2 teaspoon dried oregano**
> **500 g/1 lb scallops**
> **2 tablespoons finely chopped fresh parsley**
> **freshly ground black pepper**
> **30 g/1 oz Gruyère cheese, grated**

method

1. Heat oil in a nonstick frying pan over a medium heat, add onion and garlic and cook, stirring, for 3-4 minutes or until onion is soft. Stir in tomatoes, thyme and oregano and bring to the boil. Reduce heat and simmer for 10 minutes or until mixture reduces and thickens.
2. Add scallops, parsley and black pepper to taste and cook for 5 minutes. Divide mixture between 4 scallop shells or shell shaped dishes, sprinkle with Gruyère cheese and cook under a preheated hot grill for 4-5 minutes or until cheese melts and is golden.

....

Serves 4

tip from the chef

The sauce for this dish should be very thick before adding the scallops as the juices from them will dilute it.

cheesy grilled mussels

a

■■□ | Cooking time: 10 minutes - Preparation time: 15 minutes

method

1. Place water in a large saucepan and bring to the boil. Add mussels (a) and cook for 5 minutes or until shells open. Discard any mussels that do not open after 5 minutes cooking. Using a slotted spoon remove mussels from liquid and set aside until cool enough to handle.
2. Remove top shells of mussels and discard. Loosen mussels in bottom shells (b) but do not remove. Place shells on griller tray.
3. To make topping, place garlic, coriander, chili, lemon rind, Parmesan cheese, breadcrumbs, butter and black pepper to taste in a bowl and mix to combine (c). Top each mussel with a little of the topping (d) and cook under a preheated grill for 3 minutes or until mussels are heated through and topping is golden.

....
Makes 24

ingredients

> **2 cups/500 ml/16 fl oz water**
> **24 mussels, scrubbed and beards removed**

cheesy topping

> **2 cloves garlic, crushed**
> **1 tablespoon finely chopped fresh coriander**
> **1 small red chili, seeded and chopped**
> **1 teaspoon finely grated lemon rind**
> **2 tablespoons grated Parmesan cheese**
> **1 cup/60 g/2 oz breadcrumbs, made from stale bread**
> **60 g/2 oz butter, melted**
> **freshly ground black pepper**

b

c

d

tuna
and prawn sushi

■■■ | Cooking time: 20 minutes - Preparation time: 35 minutes

ingredients
> **2 teaspoons wasabi powder**
> **12 large cooked prawns, shelled and deveined, tails left intact**
> **125 g/4 oz fresh tuna**
> **1 sheet nori, cut into strips (optional)**
> **soy sauce**

sushi rice
> **500 g/1 lb short grain rice**
> **2¹/₂ cups/600 ml/1 pt water**
> **2 tablespoons sweet sake or sherry**
> **4 tablespoons rice vinegar**
> **2 tablespoons sugar**
> **¹/₂ teaspoon salt**

method
1. To make sushi rice, wash rice several times in cold water and set aside to drain for 30 minutes. Place rice and water in a large saucepan and bring to the boil, cover and cook, without stirring, over a low heat for 15 minutes. Remove pan from heat and set aside for 10 minutes.
2. Place sake or sherry, vinegar, sugar and salt in a small saucepan and bring to the boil. Remove pan from heat and set aside to cool. Turn rice out into a large shallow dish, pour over vinegar mixture (a) and toss gently until rice has cooled to room temperature. Take a tablespoon of rice in your hand and gently squeeze it to form a neat oval (b). Place on a serving platter and repeat with remaining rice to make 24 ovals.
3. Mix wasabi powder with a few drops of water to make a smooth paste and dab a little on each rice oval.
4. Split prawns on the underside, taking care not to cut all the way through, and flatten them out. Top twelve rice ovals with prawns.
5. Cut tuna into twelve 2 x 4 cm/³/₄ x 1¹/₂ in strips each 5 mm/¹/₄ in thick. Top remaining rice ovals with tuna strips. Wrap a strip of nori, if using, around each sushi. Serve with soy sauce for dipping.

tip from the chef
Strips of spring onion can be used in place of the nori if you wish. Wasabi is a very hot horseradish powder. It is available from Asian food stores.

Makes 24

a

b

bouillabaisse

■□□ | Cooking time: 15 minutes - Preparation time: 20 minutes

method

1. Heat oil in a large saucepan, add onions, fennel and garlic and stir over a medium heat for 5-6 minutes or until onions are soft. Stir in stock, tomato purée, tomatoes, thyme, bay leaves and turmeric, and bring to simmering.
2. Add fish, prawns, crabs and mussels and cook for 5 minutes or until seafood is just cooked. Discard any mussels that do not open after 5 minutes. Stir in basil and season to taste with black pepper. To serve, place seafood on a large serving platter and ladle soup into a tureen.

....
Serves 8

ingredients

> **2 tablespoons olive oil**
> **3 onions, chopped**
> **1 fennel bulb, thinly sliced**
> **4 cloves garlic, crushed**
> **4 cups/1 litre/1³/₄ pt chicken stock**
> **440 g/14 oz canned tomato purée**
> **2 x 440 g/14 oz canned tomatoes, undrained and mashed**
> **1 tablespoon chopped fresh thyme or 1 teaspoon dried thyme**
> **2 bay leaves**
> **¹/₂ teaspoon ground turmeric**
> **750 g/1¹/₂ lb firm white fish fillets, cut into 5 cm/2 in pieces**
> **500 g/1 lb uncooked prawns, shelled and deveined, tails left intact**
> **4 uncooked crabs, halved**
> **500 g/1 lb mussels, scrubbed and beards removed**
> **3 tablespoons chopped fresh basil**
> **freshly ground black pepper**

tip from the chef

More of a stew than a soup, bouillabaisse is one of the best known and most popular fish soups. It can be made using whatever seafood is available so use this recipe as a guide only. For a complete meal accompany bouillabaisse with crusty French bread and a glass of dry white wine.

tomato
and shellfish soup

■■□ | Cooking time: 50 minutes - Preparation time: 20 minutes

ingredients

> **2 tablespoons olive oil**
> **2 red onions, cut into rings**
> **8 large tomatoes, chopped**
> **2 cloves garlic, crushed**
> **1 teaspoon cracked black peppercorns**
> **1 tablespoon chopped fresh oregano**
> **1 tablespoon chopped fresh parsley**
> **1 tablespoon chopped fresh basil**
> **3 cups chicken stock**
> **1/2 cup tomato purée**
> **155 g/5 oz vermicelli noodles**
> **1 cup assorted shellfish, cooked**

method

1. Heat oil in a large deep frying pan, add onions and cook for 3 minutes. Add tomatoes, garlic, pepper and herbs and simmer until tomatoes are soft.
2. Add 2 cups of chicken stock to tomato mixture, boil, reduce heat and simmer for 30 minutes. Push mixture through a sieve into a large saucepan.
3. Add remaining stock and tomato purée to mixture, bring to the boil, add vermicelli and cook until tender. Stir in shellfish just before serving.

Serves 4-6

tip from the chef
It is ideal to serve this delightful soup with a sauvignon blanc wine.

creamy
mussel soup

■□□ | Cooking time: 15 minutes - Preparation time: 15 minutes

method

1. Place wine, chili paste (sambal oelek), lemon juice and garlic in a large saucepan and bring to the boil. Add mussels and cook for 5 minutes or until shells open. Discard any unopened mussels. Using a slotted spoon remove mussels from liquid and set aside.
2. Strain liquid through a fine sieve and return to a clean pan. Stir cream into wine mixture and bring to the boil. Reduce heat and simmer for 10 minutes.
3. Remove mussels from shells and stir into soup mixture. Add dill and season to taste with black pepper. Serve immediately.

Serves 4

ingredients

> 2^1/$_2$ cups/600 ml/1 pt dry white wine
> 1 teaspoon chili paste (sambal oelek)
> 2 tablespoons lemon juice
> 2 cloves garlic, crushed
> 500 g/1 lb mussels, scrubbed and beards removed
> 1^1/$_2$ cups/375 ml/ 12 fl oz double cream
> 1 tablespoon chopped fresh dill
> freshly ground black pepper

tip from the chef

Remember, any mussels that do not open their shells after 5 minutes of cooking should be discarded; they are bad.

mixed
seafood salad

■■☐ | Cooking time: 10 minutes - Preparation time: 15 minutes

ingredients

> **2 cups white wine**
> **375 g/³/4 lb mussels**
> **315 g/10 oz pipis**
> **250 g/¹/2 lb scallops**
> **155 g/5 oz squid, cut into rings**
> **200 g/6¹/2 oz medium cooked prawns, shelled and deveined, tails left intact**
> **¹/2 cup olive oil**
> **3 tablespoons lemon juice**
> **2 tablespoons chopped fresh parsley**
> **1 tablespoon chopped fresh oregano**

method

1. Combine wine, mussels and pipis in a large saucepan, cover, bring to the boil. Cook until shells open. Remove with a slotted spoon and place in a large bowl.
2. Add scallops and squid to the boiling liquid and cook for 2 minutes. Remove with slotted spoon and add to mussels and pipis. Add prawns.
3. Pour combined olive oil, lemon juice, parsley and oregano over seafood and chill for several hours before serving.

Serves 6

tip from the chef
If you wish to serve this salad as a cocktail appetizer, place some spoonfuls of mixture over toasts.

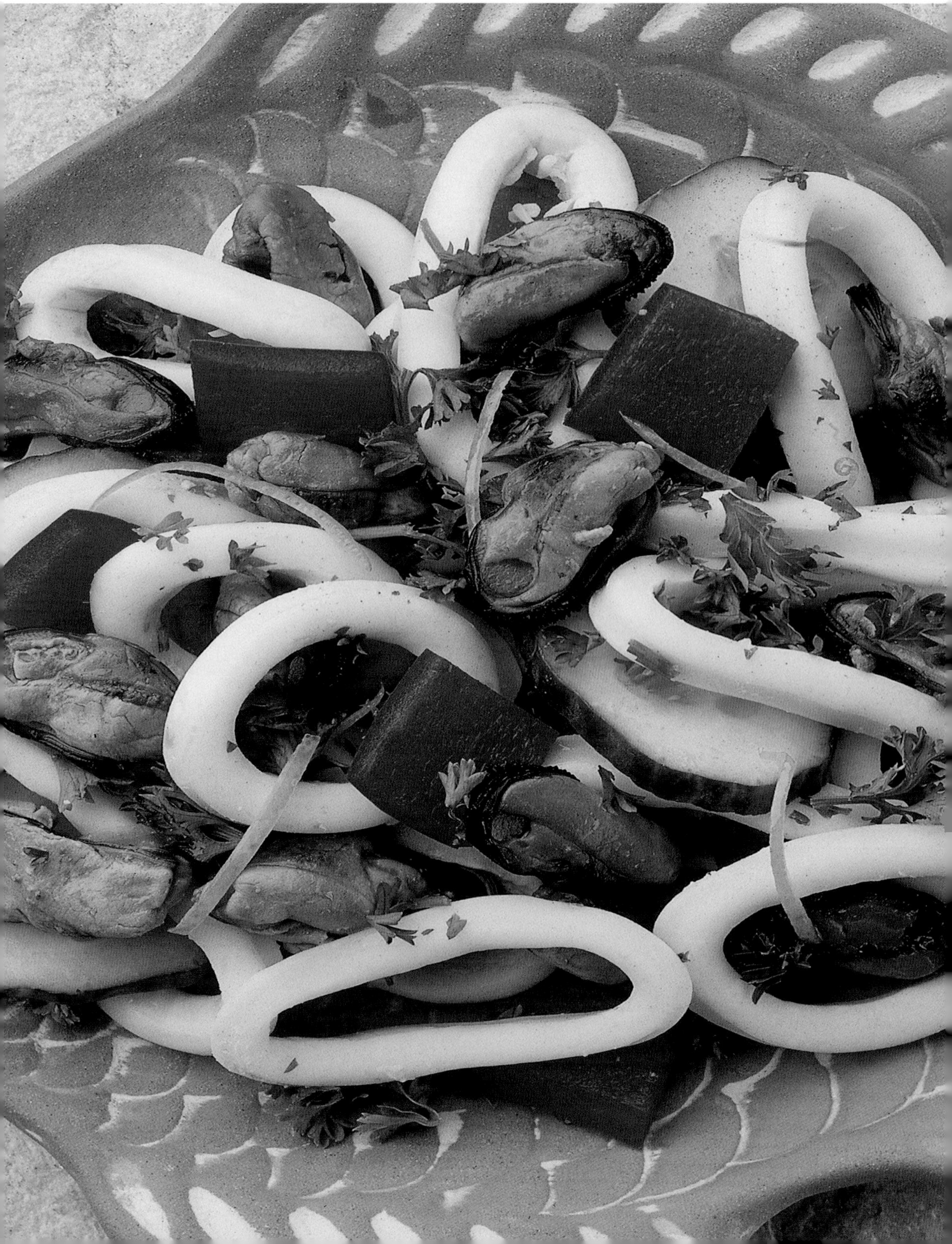

smoked
mussel and squid salad

■□□ | Cooking time: 10 minutes - Preparation time: 15 minutes

method

1. Place water, wine and lemon juice in a medium frying pan and bring to the boil.
2. Slice squid into neat rings and add to frying pan, cook for 5 minutes. Remove from heat and leave to cool in juices.
3. Drain squid and arrange on serving plate with mussels, cucumber, parsley and orange rind.
4. Dress salad with combined walnut oil, vinegar and lime juice.

Serves 4

ingredients

> 1 cup water
> 1 1/2 cups dry white wine
> 1/4 cup lemon juice
> 250 g/1/2 lb cleaned baby squid
> 1 cup smoked mussels, drained
> 1 cucumber, sliced
> 1 tablespoon chopped parsley
> rind from 1 orange, sliced into thin strips
> 3 tablespoons walnut oil
> 1 tablespoon wine vinegar
> 1 tablespoon lime juice

tip from the chef

Squid, one of the major marine food resources and possibly the most important of those which are not yet fully exploited, occur in all oceans and seas except the Black Sea.

spanish
seafood salad

■■□ | Cooking time: 35 minutes - Preparation time: 30 minutes

method

1. Place stock in a large saucepan and bring to the boil. Add prawns and cook for 1-2 minutes or until prawns change color. Remove and set aside. Add lobster tail (if using) and cook for 5 minutes or until lobster changes color and is cooked. Remove and set aside. Add mussels and cook until shells open —discard any mussels that do not open after 5 minutes. Remove and set aside. Strain stock and reserve. Peel and devein prawns, leaving tails intact. Refrigerate seafood until just prior to serving.

2. Heat oil in a large saucepan, add onion and cook for 4-5 minutes or until soft. Add ham, rice and saffron and cook, stirring, for 2 minutes. Add reserved stock and bring to the boil. Reduce heat, cover and simmer for 15 minutes or until liquid is absorbed and rice is cooked and dry. Stir in peas and red pepper and set aside to cool. Cover and refrigerate for at least 2 hours.

3. To make dressing, place oil, vinegar, mayonnaise, garlic, parsley and black pepper in a food processor or blender and process to combine.

4. To serve, place seafood and rice in a large salad bowl, spoon over dressing and toss to combine.

....
Serves 8

ingredients

> **4 cups/1 liter/1³/₄ pt chicken stock**
> **500 g/1 lb uncooked large prawns**
> **1 uncooked lobster tail (optional)**
> **500 g/l lb mussels in shells, cleaned**
> **2 tablespoons olive oil**
> **1 onion, chopped**
> **2 ham steaks, cut into 1 cm/¹/₂ in cubes**
> **2 cups/440 g/14 oz rice**
> **¹/₂ teaspoon saffron powder**
> **125 g/4 oz fresh or frozen peas**
> **1 red pepper, diced**

garlic dressing

> **¹/₂ cup/125 ml/4 fl oz olive oil**
> **¹/₄ cup/60 ml/2 fl oz white wine vinegar**
> **3 tablespoons mayonnaise**
> **2 cloves garlic, crushed**
> **2 tablespoons chopped fresh parsley**
> **freshly ground black pepper**

tip from the chef
This creative salad is the cold version of paella, the world famous Spanish recipe.

marinated
seafood salad

■□□ | Cooking time: 15 minutes - Preparation time: 15 minutes

method

1. Bring wine and lemon juice to the boil in a medium frying pan. Add chili, scallops and squid rings and cook for 2 minutes. Transfer scallops and squid to a medium bowl with a slotted spoon.
2. Add 1 cup of water to the pan juices and bring to the boil. Add mussels, cover and steam for 5 minutes or until shells have opened. Remove mussels with a slotted spoon and leave to cool.
3. Remove mussels from shells and add to scallops and squid.
4. Bring pan juices to the boil, simmer and reduce to 1/2 cup.
5. Add prawns to cooked seafood and pour over combined olive oil, lime juice, basil and reduced pan juices. Marinate salad in refrigerator 4 hours before serving.

ingredients

> 3/4 cup dry white wine
> 1/4 cup lemon juice
> 2 teaspoons finely chopped chili
> 250 g/1/2 lb scallops
> 250 g/1/2 lb squid, cut into rings
> 500 g/1 lb mussels
> 500 g/1 lb cooked medium prawns, shelled and deveined, tails left intact
> 1/4 cup olive oil
> 3 tablespoons lime juice
> 1 tablespoon chopped fresh basil

....

Serves 6

tip from the chef

It is highly suggested to present this salad over a bed of green leaves.

lobster salad

■□□ | Cooking time: 0 minute - Preparation time: 20 minutes

ingredients

> **2 lobster tails, cooked and shells removed**
> **1 radicchio, leaves separated**
> **1 lettuce, leaves separated**
> **100 g/3¹/₂ oz snow pea sprouts or watercress**
> **1 orange, peeled and segmented**
> **250 g/8 oz strawberries**

raspberry dressing

> **125 g/4 oz fresh or frozen raspberries**
> **2 tablespoons raspberry vinegar**
> **2 tablespoons vegetable oil**
> **1 teaspoon chopped fresh mint**
> **1 tablespoon sugar**

method

1. Cut lobster tails into 1 cm/¹/₂ in thick medallions and set aside.
2. Arrange radicchio and lettuce leaves, sprouts or watercress, orange segments, strawberries and lobster attractively on a serving platter. Cover and refrigerate.
3. To make dressing, place raspberries in a food processor or blender and process until puréed. Push purée through a sieve to remove seeds. Place raspberry purée, vinegar, oil, mint and sugar in a small bowl and mix to combine. Drizzle dressing over salad and serve immediately.

Serves 4 as a main course

tip from the chef

To cook lobster, place dead lobster in a saucepan of cold water, bring slowly to the boil and boil, allowing 8 minutes per 500 g/1 lb of lobster. To kill a live lobster, either drown it in fresh water or freeze it.

baked snapper
with pineapple seasoning

■ ■ ■ | Cooking time: 50 minutes - Preparation time: 25 minutes

method

1. Soak cracked wheat in boiling water for 20 minutes; strain; drain well. In a medium bowl combine wheat, half the pineapple pieces, half the spring onions, half the pepper, wheatgerm and egg; mix well.
2. Wash fish under cold water. Fill cavity of fish with pineapple mixture. Place fish on a greased oven tray, brush with oil and bake in moderate oven for 30 minutes.
3. In a small saucepan combine chicken stock, cornflour, soy sauce and pineapple juice. Stir sauce over a low heat until mixture boils and thickens, add remaining pineapple pieces, spring onions and pepper, serve over fish.

Serves 4

ingredients

> 2 tablespoons cracked wheat
> 450 g/14 oz canned unsweetened pineapple pieces, drained, and 1/2 cup juice reserved
> 2 spring onions, chopped
> 1/2 red pepper, chopped
> 1 tablespoon wheatgerm
> 1 egg
> 1 whole snapper, cleaned
> oil, for brushing fish
> 1/2 cup chicken stock
> 1 tablespoon cornflour
> 1 teaspoon light soy sauce

tip from the chef

It is an extremely original plate that combines very exotic flavors. When filling the fish, be careful not to use too much stuffing so that it does not overflow while being cooked.

fish
with orange butter

■ ■ ■ | Cooking time: 35 minutes - Preparation time: 30 minutes

ingredients

> **60 g/2 oz butter**
> **4 spring onions, chopped**
> **1 clove garlic, crushed**
> **1 orange, peeled and segmented**
> **2 tablespoons chopped fresh parsley**
> **1 cup/60 g/2 oz breadcrumbs, made from stale bread**
> **freshly ground black pepper**
> **1 kg/2 lb whole small fish, such as snapper or bream, cleaned**

orange butter

> **125 g/4 oz butter, softened**
> **3 teaspoons finely grated orange rind**
> **1 tablespoon orange juice**
> **2 teaspoons tomato sauce**

method

1. Preheat barbecue to a medium heat.
2. Melt butter in a large frying pan and cook spring onions and garlic for 1-2 minutes. Remove pan from heat and stir in orange segments (a), parsley, breadcrumbs and black pepper to taste. Fill cavity of each fish with breadcrumb mixture. Close cavity and secure with wooden toothpicks.
3. Cut a piece of aluminum foil large enough to completely enclose the fish. Lightly grease foil and place fish in center. Fold foil over fish to enclose completely and seal by rolling edges together. Cook fish on preheated barbecue grill, turning several times, for 25-30 minutes or until flesh flakes when tested with a fork.
4. To make orange butter, place butter, orange rind, orange juice, tomato sauce and black pepper to taste in a bowl and mix to combine. Place butter mixture on a piece of aluminum foil (b) and form into a sausage shape. Wrap foil around butter and refrigerate until firm. Sliced and serve with fish.

....
Serves 4

tip from the chef

This fish is also delicious baked in the oven at 180°C/350°F/Gas 4 for 30-35 minutes.

a

b

fish
baked in paper

■ ■ □ | Cooking time: 35 minutes - Preparation time: 20 minutes

method

1. Heat oil in a large frying pan and stir-fry zucchini, red peppers and lemon rind over a medium heat for 2-3 minutes. Remove pan from heat.
2. Cut 4 pieces of nonstick baking paper large enough to enclose each fish. Divide vegetable mixture between pieces of paper and top each with a fish. Sprinkle with lemon juice and fold baking paper around fish to enclose. Seal edges by rolling together tightly.
3. Bake at 180°C/350°F/Gas 4 for 30 minutes or until flesh flakes when tested with a fork.

....
Serves 4

ingredients

> **1 tablespoon olive oil**
> **4 large zucchini, cut into strips**
> **2 red peppers, cut into strips**
> **rind from 1/2 lemon, cut into strips**
> **4 small whole fish, such as bream, sea perch, snapper or pompano, cleaned**
> **2 tablespoons lemon juice**

tip from the chef

Cooking fish in paper prevents it from drying out and nearly all types of fish are suitable to cook this way. The fish is cooked when the paper browns and puffs up. The best part of cooking fish in this way is when you open the parcel and release the rich aroma that has formed during cooking. The French call this method of cooking en papillote.

steamed fish

■□ □ I Cooking time: 15 minutes - Preparation time: 15 minutes

ingredients

> **2 small whole fish, such as snapper or bream, cleaned**
> **1 tablespoon finely chopped fresh ginger**
> **1 tablespoon soy sauce**
> **1 teaspoon sugar**
> **1 tablespoon white vinegar**
> **2 rashers bacon, cut into strips**
> **1 small carrot, cut into thin strips**
> **4 spring onions, cut into 3 cm/1¼ in lengths**

method

1. Place fish in a shallow glass or ceramic dish. Combine ginger, soy sauce, sugar and vinegar. Pour mixture over fish, cover and set aside to marinate for 30 minutes.
2. Line a bamboo steamer with nonstick baking paper. Place fish in steamer, pour over marinade and sprinkle with bacon, carrot and spring onions.
3. Cover steamer, place over a wok of simmering water and steam for 10-15 minutes or until fish flakes when tested with a fork.

. . . .
Serves 2

tip from the chef

The Chinese always serve whole fish with the head pointing towards the guest of honor. It is believed that this assures him or her of good fortune.

bream
with grapefruit

■□□ | Cooking time: 25 minutes - Preparation time: 15 minutes

method

1. Place each fish on foil to wrap, brush with combined melted butter, garlic, lime juice and grapefruit juice. Wrap up in foil and bake in moderate oven for 25 minutes.

2. Decorate with grapefruit slices and fresh dill. Serve with blanched vegetables if desired.

....
Serves 4

ingredients

> **4 medium bream, cleaned**
> **$^1/_2$ cup melted butter**
> **1 clove garlic, crushed**
> **2 tablespoons freshly squeezed lime juice**
> **4 tablespoons freshly squeezed grapefruit juice**
> **1 grapefruit, sliced**
> **1 tablespoon chopped fresh dill**

tip from the chef

This fish can be served either hot or cold. To eat it cold, shred the flesh, mix with greens and drizzle with a vinaigrette made with oil, the juices of the same citric fruits used for the cooking and some seasoning.

whiting with sweet and sour rice

■■□ | Cooking time: 40 minutes - Preparation time: 20 minutes

ingredients

> **4 whole whiting, cleaned**
> **2 tablespoons lemon juice**
> **2 tablespoons olive oil**

rice

> **4 tablespoons olive oil**
> **1 large onion, chopped**
> **1/4 cup pine nuts**
> **3/4 cup long grain rice**
> **1 tablespoon grated fresh ginger**
> **1/2 red pepper, seeded and chopped finely**
> **1/4 cup baby corn cobs, sliced**
> **3 tablespoons sugar**
> **2 tablespoons lemon juice**
> **1 tablespoon fresh parsley, chopped**

method

1. Wash the fish and season inside and out. Brush the outside with combined lemon juice and olive oil. Wrap each fish in foil and bake in moderate oven for 20 minutes.
2. To make rice, heat oil in a large frying pan, add onion and pine nuts and cook for 2 minutes. Add rice, ginger, pepper and corn, pour 2 cups of water into mixture and bring to the boil. Simmer for 15 minutes or until rice is tender and water has evaporated (you may need to add more water).
3. Stir in sugar and lemon juice and cook for a further 2 minutes. Stir in parsley and divide rice between 4 plates.
4. Remove fish from foil and place on top of rice. Garnish with parsley if desired.

....
Serves 4

tip from the chef
In order to give the rice a special flavor, add 3 spoonfuls of raisins.

warm
mullet niçoise

■■ ■■ □ | Cooking time: 25 minutes - Preparation time: 20 minutes

method

1. Cut the heads off the fish and wash thoroughly. Place fish in a single layer in a greased baking tray. Brush each fish generously with olive oil and wrap foil around the tails.
2. Mix together tomatoes, onion, garlic, olives and parsley and place on and around the fish in the baking tray.
3. Pour wine over the top and bake in moderate oven for 20-25 minutes or until fish is cooked through. Serve each fish with the tomato onion mixture.

ingredients

> **4 whole mullet, cleaned**
> **¹/4 cup olive oil**
> **3 tomatoes, chopped into small cubes**
> **1 onion, chopped**
> **2 cloves garlic, chopped**
> **10 black olives, pitted and chopped**
> **2 tablespoons parsley, chopped**
> **1 cup dry white wine**

....

Serves 4

tip from the chef

An excellent resource to intensify its flavor is to sprinkle the fish with grated Parmesan cheese.

jewfish
steaks with dill butter

■□□ | Cooking time: 10 minutes - Preparation time: 15 minutes

ingredients

> **4 jewfish steaks**
> **3 tablespoons freshly squeezed lemon juice**
> **1 teaspoon chili paste (sambal oelek)**
> **3 tablespoons white wine**
> **3 tablespoons oil**
> **4 egg yolks**
> **2 tablespoons freshly squeezed lime juice**
> **60 g/2 oz butter, melted and boiling**
> **1 tablespoon chopped dill**

method

1. Brush jewfish with combined lemon juice, chili paste, wine and oil and cook under a moderately preheated grill for 5 minutes each side or until cooked through.
2. Blend egg yolks with lime juice in a food processor or blender for 1 minute. While the motor is running, add the bubbling butter (it is important that the butter is boiling while pouring into egg yolk mixture) and process for a further 1 minute. Stir in dill and serve over jewfish.

Serves 4

tip from the chef

These filets can also be cooked in the oven or in a barbecue.

fillet of fish
with mustard sauce

a

■ ■ □ | Cooking time: 15 minutes - Preparation time: 15 minutes

method

1. Melt butter in a large frying pan over medium heat. Add zucchini, red peppers and celery (a) and sauté for 2 minutes. Remove with a slotted spoon and place in foil in a low oven to keep warm.
2. Add fish fillets to pan (b), cook for 2 minutes on each side or until cooked through. Transfer fillets to a baking dish, cover with foil and keep warm in oven.
3. Add cream to pan, bring to the boil and reduce to 3/4 cup. Add mustard (c) and mix well.
4. Divide vegetables between serving plates, place two fish fillets on top of vegetables, top with mustard sauce (d) and serve immediately.

ingredients

> **4 tablespoons butter**
> **4 zucchini, cut into thin strips**
> **2 red peppers, seeded and cut into thin strips**
> **2 celery sticks, cut into thin strips**
> **8 white fish fillets**
> **1 1/2 cups cream**
> **1 tablespoon whole grain mustard**

....
Serves 4

tip from the chef

Two tablespoons of Dijon mustard can be used instead of the whole grain mustard.

b

c

d

john
dory rolls

■■■ I Cooking time: 25 minutes - Preparation time: 25 minutes

ingredients

> ¹/4 cup/60 ml/2 fl oz
  lemon juice
> 2 cloves garlic, crushed
> freshly ground black
  pepper
> 8 x 60-75 g/2-2¹/2 oz
  John Dory fillets
> 16 spinach leaves, stems
  removed
> 1 tablespoon snipped
  fresh chives

lemon sauce

> 2 tablespoons lemon juice
> ¹/2 cup/125 ml/4 fl oz
  evaporated milk
> 2 teaspoons cornflour

method

1. Place lemon juice, garlic and black pepper to taste in a small bowl and whisk to combine. Brush each fillet with lemon juice mixture, then top with 2 spinach leaves, folding them to fit the fillets.
2. Roll up fillets and secure with wooden toothpicks. Place rolls in a lightly oiled, shallow ovenproof dish and bake at 180°C/350°F/Gas 4 for 20 minutes or until fish is cooked. Remove fish from dish, set aside and keep warm. Reserve cooking juices.
3. To make sauce, place the reserved cooking juices, lemon juice, evaporated milk, cornflour and black pepper to taste in a small saucepan and cook over a medium heat, stirring constantly, for 3-4 minutes or until sauce boils and thickens slightly. Spoon sauce over rolls, sprinkle with chives and serve immediately.

....
Serves 4

tip from the chef

Lemon always makes fish taste better. For this recipe, a chardonnay wine with citric notes and wooden touches is the most appropriate beverage.

a

b

pink
and white fish mosaic

■■■ I Cooking time: 25 minutes - Preparation time: 25 minutes

method

1. Cut each white fish fillet lengthwise into 4 strips, each measuring 15 x 2 cm/6 x ³/₄ in. Sprinkle with 1 tablespoon lemon juice and season with white pepper. Wrap each strip in blanched spinach leaves (a) and set aside. Cut salmon fillets crosswise into 16 strips the same size as the white fish ones. Sprinkle with remaining lemon juice and season with white pepper.

2. Weave 4 strips of each fish into a square to form a checkerboard pattern (b) on pieces of foil. Trim ends if necessary. Place a wire rack and 2.5 cm/1 in water in a large frying pan and bring to the boil. Place fish on wire rack and steam for 6-8 minutes.

3. To make sauce, melt half the butter in a saucepan and cook spring onions, garlic and sage for 2 minutes. Add spinach and cook for 5 minutes longer or until wilted. Add stock, bay leaf and wine and boil until mixture reduces by half. Remove bay leaf.

4. Place sauce in a food processor or blender and process until smooth. Pass through a fine sieve into a clean saucepan. Stir in cream and cook over a low heat for 5 minutes. Whisk in small pieces of remaining butter. Season with black pepper and serve with fish squares.

....

Serves 4

ingredients

> **4 large firm white fish fillets**
> **2 tablespoons lemon juice**
> **freshly ground white pepper**
> **16 large spinach leaves, blanched, stalks removed**
> **2 salmon fillets**

spinach sauce

> **45 g/l ¹/₂ oz butter**
> **2 spring onions, chopped**
> **1 clove garlic, crushed**
> **2 fresh sage leaves**
> **200 g/6¹/₂ oz young spinach leaves**
> **2 cups/500 ml/16 fl oz fish stock**
> **1 bay leaf**
> **¹/₂ cup/125 ml/4 fl oz dry white wine**
> **1 cup/250 ml/8 fl oz double cream**
> **freshly ground black pepper**

tip from the chef

This recipe can be easily cooked in the microwave. Thus, place the prepared fish squares on a piece of nonstick baking paper rather than the aluminum foil, place in a shallow microwave-safe dish, cover and cook on High (100%) for 4-5 minutes or until fish is cooked.

a

b

c

seafood
terrine

■■□ | Cooking time: 30 minutes - Preparation time: 20 minutes

method

1. Cut fish into small pieces and process (a) to a purée in a blender or food processor. Push purée through a sieve into a bowl set over ice. Mix in egg whites and cream (b) until mixture becomes bulky. Add lemon juice, mix well.
2. Brush a loaf pan with oil. Cut a long strip of non-stick baking paper the narrow width of the base of the pan and run it down one end, along the base and up the other end. Brush with oil (c).
3. Divide fish mixture into 2 bowls. Mix prawns into one bowl. Spread half the plain fish purée over the base of the pan. Lay zucchini slices on top, then spread half of the prawn mixture over the zucchini. Repeat layers of zucchini, prawn mixture (d) and plain fish purée, cover with foil and place pan in a roasting dish.
4. Pour hot water around to come about half way up the sides. Cook in moderate oven for 30 minutes. Allow terrine to cool for 10 minutes in pan before turning out.

....

Serves 8

ingredients

> **500g/1 lb boneless white fish fillets**
> **2 egg whites**
> **1¹/₂ cups thickened cream**
> **3 tablespoons lemon juice**
> **1 cup cooked medium prawns, shelled and deveined, chopped**
> **3 large zucchini, cut into thin slices**

tip from the chef

If you prefer a more colorful terrine, blanched carrots can replace one of the zucchini layers.

d

barbecued
stuffed squid

▪▪☐ | Cooking time: 5 minutes - Preparation time: 15 minutes

method

1. Preheat barbecue to a high heat.
2. To make filling, place breadcrumbs, cheese, olives, tomatoes, lemon juice, oregano and black pepper to taste in bowl and mix to combine.
3. Spoon filling into squid tubes and secure opening with a wooden toothpick or cocktail stick. Lightly brush with oil and cook on barbecue for 1 minute each side or until squid is white and opaque.

....

Serves 8

ingredients

> **20 baby squid tubes, cleaned**
> **olive oil**

feta and olive filling

> **1 cup/60 g/2 oz breadcrumbs, made from stale bread**
> **315 g/10 oz feta cheese, crumbled**
> **3 tablespoons chopped black olives**
> **2 tablespoons chopped sun-dried tomatoes**
> **1/4 cup/60 ml/2 fl oz lemon juice**
> **1 tablespoon chopped fresh oregano**
> **freshly ground black pepper**

tip from the chef

When filling the squid, take care not to overfill them or they will burst during cooking. As soon as the squid come in contact with the hot barbecue they will shrink. Only the squid bodies or tubes are used for this recipe, reserve tentacles for another use. It is sometimes possible to purchase cleaned baby squid in which case they could be used for this recipe.

prawn
skewers

■□□ | Cooking time: 5 minutes - Preparation time: 10 minutes

ingredients

> **500 g/1 lb large uncooked prawns, shelled and deveined, tails left intact**
> **2 teaspoons sesame oil**
> **1 tablespoon soy sauce**
> **1 tablespoon vegetable oil**
> **1 teaspoon honey**
> **1 clove garlic, crushed**
> **freshly ground black pepper**

method

1. Thread prawns onto oiled bamboo skewers (a).
2. Place sesame oil, soy sauce, vegetable oil, honey, garlic and black pepper to taste in a small bowl and whisk to combine. Brush prawns with oil mixture.
3. Cook skewers under a preheated grill or on a preheated barbecue, brushing frequently with oil mixture (b), for 3-4 minutes each side or until prawns change color and are cooked.
4. Serve skewers on a bed of steamed rice.

....

Serves 4

tip from the chef

When storing prawns, leave them in their shells. The shell acts as a natural insulator and helps retain moisture and flavor. Cooked prawns should be stored in the refrigerator in an airtight container or plastic food bag for no longer than 3 days. Uncooked prawns are best stored in water in an airtight container for up to 3 days. The water prevents oxidation.

a

b

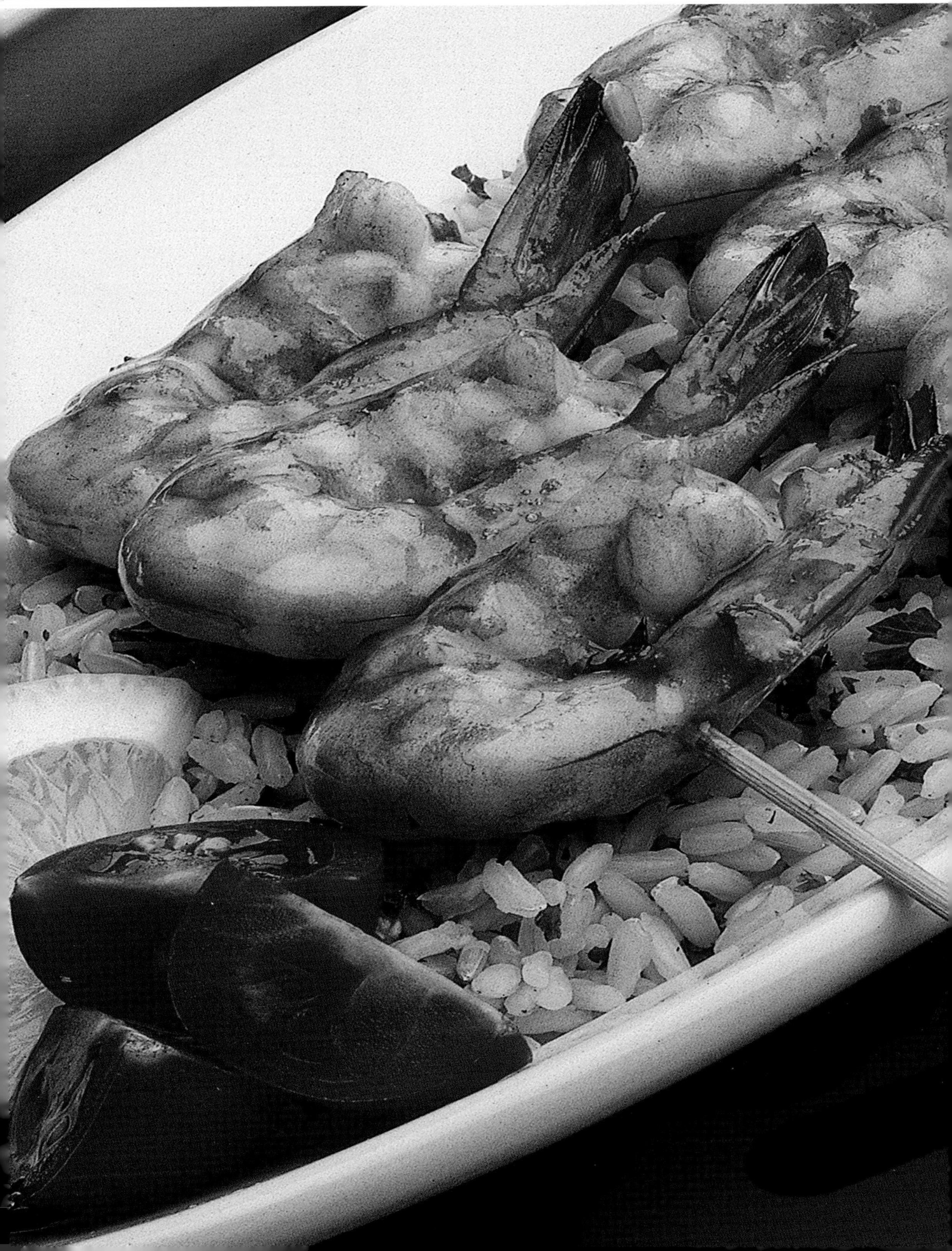

barbecued
marinated prawns

■ □ □ | Cooking time: 5 minutes - Preparation time: 10 minutes

method

1. Preheat barbecue to a medium heat.
2. To make marinade, place chilies, garlic, oregano, parsley, oil, vinegar and black pepper to taste in a bowl and mix to combine. Add prawns, toss to coat and marinate for 10 minutes.
3. Drain prawns and cook on oiled barbecue for 1-2 minutes each side or until prawns just change color.

....
Serves 8

ingredients

> **1 kg/2 lb uncooked medium prawns, shelled and deveined, tails left intact**

chili and herb marinade

> **2 fresh red chilies, chopped**
> **2 cloves garlic, crushed**
> **1 tablespoon chopped fresh oregano**
> **1 tablespoon chopped fresh parsley**
> **1/4 cup/60 ml/2 fl oz olive oil**
> **2 tablespoons balsamic vinegar**
> **freshly ground black pepper**

tip from the chef

For an attractive presentation, line a serving platter with trimmed spring onions and pile the prawns on top. The juices from the prawns will flavor the spring onions and you will have another delicious pre-meal nibble.

seafood
combination

■■□ | Cooking time: 15 minutes - Preparation time: 15 minutes

ingredients

> ¼ cup/60 ml/2 fl oz vegetable oil
> 375 g/12 oz uncooked large prawns, shelled and deveined
> 250 g/8 oz squid rings
> 250 g/8 oz firm white fish fillets, cut into cubes
> 125 g/4 oz scallops
> 1 red pepper, cut into strips
> 250 g/8 oz snow peas
> 220 g/7 oz canned sliced bamboo shoots, drained
> 2 cloves garlic, crushed
> 2 teaspoons grated fresh ginger
> 2 teaspoons cornflour
> ½ cup/125 ml/4 fl oz chicken stock
> 1 teaspoon sesame oil
> 2 teaspoons soy sauce

method

1. Heat 2 tablespoons vegetable oil in a wok or frying pan, add prawns, squid, fish and scallops (a) and stir-fry for 2-3 minutes. Remove seafood from pan and set aside.
2. Add remaining vegetable oil to pan, heat and add red pepper, snow peas, bamboo shoots, garlic and ginger (b) and stir-fry for 4-5 minutes or until red pepper and snow peas are tender.
3. Combine cornflour, chicken stock, sesame oil and soy sauce and stir into pan (c). Cook, stirring constantly, until sauce boils and thickens. Return seafood to pan (d) and cook for 2-3 minutes or until heated through. Serve immediately.

Serves 4

tip from the chef
With their quick cooking times, fish and seafood are perfect for stir-frying.

a

b

c

d

lime-battered
seafood

■■■□ | Cooking time: 5 minutes - Preparation time: 20 minutes

method

1. To make batter, place flour in a bowl and gradually stir in lime juice and soda water. Mix well to combine, then stir in lime rind. Set aside.
2. To make mayonnaise, place egg yolks, lemon juice and mustard in a food processor or blender and process to combine. With machine running, slowly pour in oil and process until mixture thickens. Stir in coriander and season to taste with black pepper.
3. Heat oil in a large deep saucepan. Dip prawns, squid rings and fish fillets in batter. Drain off excess batter and cook a few at a time in hot oil, until golden. Remove from pan and drain on absorbent kitchen paper. Serve with mayonnaise for dipping.

....
Serves 4

ingredients

> **oil for deep-frying**
> **8 large uncooked prawns, shelled and deveined, tails left intact**
> **60 g/2 oz squid rings**
> **4 x 90 g/3 oz firm white fish fillets**

lime batter

> **1 1/2 cups/185 g/6 oz flour, sifted**
> **1/2 cup/125 ml/4 fl oz lime juice**
> **1 cup/250 ml/8 fl oz soda water**
> **2 teaspoons finely grated lime rind**

coriander mayonnaise

> **3 egg yolks**
> **2 tablespoons lemon juice**
> **1/4 teaspoon dry mustard**
> **1 cup/250 ml/8 fl oz vegetable oil**
> **1 tablespoon finely chopped fresh coriander**
> **freshly ground black pepper**

tip from the chef

Never before have fish and chips been this good. Make your own chips and no one will be able to resist. When heating oil for deep-frying, check the temperature by dropping a cube of bread into the hot oil. The oil is the right temperature when it will brown the bread cube in 50 seconds.

notes

Chef
express

sizzling
barbecue

table of contents

introduction

Before you start enjoying the tempting recipes in this book, it is advisable for you to know that there are many different barbecues available. The one you choose will depend on your budget, how many people you regularly feed and whether barbecuing is usually a planned or an impromptu affair.

sizzling barbecues
introduction

Gas barbecues

These contain lava rocks which are heated by gas burners. The lava rocks evenly distribute the heat and if you have a barbecue with multiple burners it is possible to have the rocks hot on one side and a medium heat on the other. Gas barbecues also require a gas bottle, which needs to be refilled on a regular basis –this is relatively inexpensive. When lighting a gas barbecue it is important to follow the manufacturer's instructions. If the barbecue does not ignite immediately, turn it off, wait for any build up of gas to disperse, then try again.

Wood or coal barbecues

The key to using these types of barbecues is patience and planning. These barbecues take up to an hour to heat, so you need to remember to light the barbecue well in advance.

Electric barbecues

These are ideal for people who want to barbecue indoors and, like gas barbecues, they produce almost instant heat.

How hot?

If your barbecue uses coal or wood, you will need to allow 30-45 minutes for coal to heat up to 45 minutes-1 hour for wood. The following is a guide for assessing the heat of these barbecues.

Hot fire

There will be a red glow showing through the thin layer of white ash and when you hold your hand 15 cm/6 in above the coals you will only be able to leave it there for 3 seconds. This fire is ideal for searing and quick cooking.

Medium fire

The red glow will be almost gone and the ash thicker and more grey in color. When you hold your hand 15 cm/6 in above the coals you will be able to leave it there for 5-7 seconds. Most barbecuing is done on this heat.

Low fire

The red glow will have disappeared and there will be a thick coating of grey ash. This heat is ideal for slow cooking of foods.

Difficulty scale

■ ☐ ☐ I Easy to do

■ ■ ☐ I Requires attention

■ ■ ■ I Requires experience

onion
and parmesan breads

■ ■ □ | Cooking time: 10 minutes - Preparation time: 2 hours 15 minutes

ingredients

> **2 teaspoons active dry yeast**
> **2¹/₂ cups/600 ml/1 pt warm water**
> **5¹/₂ cups/700 g/1 lb 7 oz flour**
> **4 spring onions, chopped**
> **4 tablespoons finely grated Parmesan cheese**
> **2 teaspoons sea salt**
> **1 tablespoon poppy seeds**

method

1. Place yeast and water in a bowl and mix to dissolve. Stand in a warm draught-free place for 5 minutes or until foamy.
2. Combine flour, spring onions, Parmesan cheese and salt in a bowl. Stir in yeast mixture (a) and continue mixing to make a smooth dough. Turn dough onto a lightly floured surface and knead for about 10 minutes or until smooth and elastic.
3. Place dough in a lightly oiled bowl and roll around bowl to coat surface with oil. Cover bowl and place in a warm draught-free place for 2 hours or until doubled in size.
4. Preheat barbecue to a medium heat. Knock dough down and knead lightly. Divide into 8 pieces. Roll out each piece on a lightly floured surface to form a round about 5 mm/¹/₄ in thick (b).
5. Pierce dough rounds all over (c), then lightly brush with oil and sprinkle with poppy seeds.
6. Place bread on barbecue grill and cook for 3-4 minutes each side. Serve warm.

....
Makes 8

tip from the chef

To make a delicious spread for these breads, process or blend 250 g/8 oz ricotta cheese until smooth. Stir in 2 tablespoons chopped fresh chives and 2 teaspoons crushed black peppercorns.

a

b

c

sage and
pancetta pizzas

■□□ I Cooking time: 10 minutes - Preparation time: 15 minutes

method

1. Preheat barbecue to a high heat. Divide pizza dough into 4 portions and roll into rounds about 1 cm/¹/₂ in thick. Lightly brush dough rounds with oil, place on barbecue grill and cook for 3-5 minutes or until well browned and crisp.
2. Flip pizza bases. Top cooked side with overlapping slices of tomatoes, pancetta and cheese. Scatter with sage leaves and black pepper to taste. Cook for 3-5 minutes longer or until base is golden and crisp and topping warm. Serve immediately.

Makes 4

ingredients

> **1 quantity pizza dough**

sage and pancetta topping

> **2 tomatoes, thinly sliced**
> **250 g/8 oz pancetta, thinly sliced**
> **250 g/8 oz bocconcini cheese, sliced**
> **2 tablespoons fresh sage leaves**
> **freshly ground black pepper**

tip from the chef

To make pizza dough, place 1 teaspoon active dry yeast, pinch sugar and 2/3 cup/170 ml/ 5¹/₂ fl oz warm water in a bowl and mix to dissolve. Stand for 5 minutes or until foamy. Place 2 cups/250 g/8 oz flour and ¹/₂ teaspoon salt in a food processor and pulse once or twice to sift. With machine running, slowly pour in yeast mixture and ¹/₄ cup/ 60 ml/2 fl oz olive oil and process to form a rough dough. Knead dough until soft and shiny. Place dough in an oiled bowl, cover with plastic food wrap and place in a warm draught-free place for 1-1¹/₂ hours or until doubled in size. Knock down and knead lightly.

chicken
and basil pizzas

■□□ | Cooking time: 15 minutes - Preparation time: 15 minutes

ingredients
> **1 quantity pizza dough (page 8)**

chicken and basil topping
> **8 plum (egg or Italian) tomatoes, thickly sliced**
> **2 boneless chicken breast fillets, cut into thick slices**
> **2 tablespoons olive oil**
> **freshly ground black pepper**
> **75 g/2¹/₂ oz marinated olives, pitted**
> **¹/₂ bunch fresh basil, shredded**
> **25 g/4 oz grated Parmesan cheese**

method
1. Preheat barbecue to a high heat. Lightly brush tomato and chicken slices with oil and season with black pepper to taste. Place on barbecue and cook for 2 minutes each side or until chicken is brown and cooked through.
2. Divide pizza dough into 8 portions and roll into rounds about 1 cm/¹/₂ in thick (a). Lightly brush dough with oil, place on barbecue grill and cook for 3-4 minutes or until golden and crisp on one side (b).
3. Flip pizza bases. Top cooked side with tomatoes and chicken, then scatter with olives and basil and sprinkle with Parmesan cheese. Cook for 3-5 minutes longer or until base is golden and crisp and topping warm (c). Serve immediately.

Makes 8

tip from the chef
Kneading is an important technique when making pizza dough. Kneading by hand will take about 5-10 minutes and the dough should be elastic, soft and shiny. Knocking after the first rising of the dough, knocks out the air bubbles which have developed during rising and ensures a good textured cooked product. **a**

b

c

char-grilled
vegetables

■ □ □ | Cooking time: 15 minutes - Preparation time: 10 minutes

method

1. Preheat barbecue to a high heat. Carefully pull back husks from sweet corn cobs, keeping them attached, and remove silk. Tie a string around the husks to form a handle. Cook sweet corn cobs in boiling water in a saucepan for 2-3 minutes or until kernels soften slightly. Drain.

2. Brush sweet corn cobs with oil. Place asparagus, zucchini, leeks, tomatoes and black pepper to taste in a bowl. Drizzle with oil and toss to coat.

3. Place all the vegetables on barbecue grill and cook, turning several times, until well browned and tender. Serve with lemon wedges.

ingredients

> **2 cobs sweet corn with husks**
> **1-2 tablespoons chili or herb oil**
> **185 g/6 oz asparagus spears**
> **2 zucchini, halved lengthwise**
> **4 baby leeks**
> **4 plum (egg or Italian) tomatoes, halved**
> **freshly ground black pepper**
> **lemon wedges**

....
Serves 6

tip from the chef

Watch a lit barbecue at all times and keep children and pets away from hot barbecues and equipment.

char-grilled
mushrooms and toast

a

■□□ | Cooking time: 10 minutes - Preparation time: 10 minutes

method

1. Preheat barbecue to a medium heat. Brush mushrooms with oil and cook on lightly oiled barbecue (a) for 4-5 minutes or until cooked.

2. Brush both sides of the bread with remaining oil and cook for 2-3 minutes each side (b) or until golden.

3. Rub one side of each bread slice with cut side of garlic clove (c). Top each slice with mushrooms, sprinkle with parsley, chives and basil. Season to taste with black pepper (d) and serve immediately.

....
Serves 2

ingredients

> **6 flat mushrooms**
> **¹/₄ cup/60 ml/2 fl oz olive oil**
> **2 thick slices of bread**
> **1 clove garlic, cut in half**
> **2 teaspoons finely chopped fresh parsley**
> **2 teaspoons snipped fresh chives**
> **1 teaspoon finely chopped fresh basil**
> **freshly ground black pepper**

tip from the chef

This delicious first course takes only minutes to cook.

b

c

d

rösti with gravlax

■□□ | Cooking time: 10 minutes - Preparation time: 10 minutes

ingredients

> ¹/₂ cup/125 g/4 oz sour cream
> 250 g/8 oz salmon gravlax
> lemon wedges

vegetable rösti

> 3 large potatoes, grated
> 2 zucchini, grated
> 2 carrots, grated
> 1 leek, shredded
> ¹/₂ cup/60 g/2 oz flour
> 3 tablespoons finely grated Parmesan cheese
> 1 tablespoon chopped fresh mint
> 1 tablespoon Dijon mustard
> 4 eggs, lightly beaten
> freshly ground black pepper

method

1. Preheat barbecue to a medium heat.
   To make rösti, place potatoes, zucchini, carrots, leek, flour, Parmesan cheese, mint, mustard, eggs and black pepper to taste in a bowl and mix to combine.
2. Place large spoonfuls of vegetable mixture on oiled barbecue plate, press with a spatula to flatten and cook for 5 minutes each side or until golden and crisp. Remove rösti from barbecue and keep warm. Repeat with remaining mixture.
3. To serve, place one or two rösti on each serving plate, top with a spoonful of sour cream, some salmon gravlax and black pepper to taste. Serve with lemon wedges.

Serves 6

tip from the chef

You will need about 440 g/14 oz potatoes for the rösti. For a cocktail party make tiny rösti and serve this tempting starter as finger food.

fish burgers with aïoli

■■□ | Cooking time: 10 minutes - Preparation time: 20 minutes

method

1. Preheat barbecue to a medium heat.
2. To make aïoli, place garlic, mustard, egg yolks and vinegar in a food processor or blender and process to combine. With machine running, slowly add olive oil in a thin stream and continue processing until mixture is thick and creamy. If mixture is too thick, add a little warm water to thin it.
3. To make marinade, place chervil or parsley, lime juice, oil and black peppercorns to taste in a shallow dish and mix to combine. Add fish, turn to coat and marinate for 5 minutes.
4. Drain fish and cook on oiled barbecue grill for 1-2 minutes each side or until flesh flakes when tested with a fork.
5. To assemble, toast buns on barbecue grill until golden. Top base of each bun with some lettuce leaves, a fish fillet and a spoonful of aïoli, then cover with top of bun.

....
Makes 4 burgers

ingredients

> **4 fillets blue-eye cod or other firm white fish**
> **4 wholemeal buns, split**
> **125 g/4 oz assorted lettuce leaves**

aïoli

> **2 cloves garlic, crushed**
> **2 teaspoons Dijon mustard**
> **3 egg yolks**
> **1 tablespoon white vinegar**
> **1 cup/250 ml/8 fl oz olive oil**

pepper and herb marinade

> **2 tablespoons chopped fresh chervil or parsley**
> **2 tablespoons lime juice**
> **1 tablespoon olive oil**
> **crushed black peppercorns**

tip from the chef

As a side dish for these burgers, toss boiled potato wedges with paprika, cumin, black pepper and oil, cook on barbecue until crisp and sprinkle with sea salt.

smoked
salmon fillet

■□□ I Cooking time: 10 minutes - Preparation time: 20 minutes

ingredients

> **125 g/4 oz hickory smoking chips**
> **1¹/₂ cups/375 ml/12 fl oz dry white wine**
> **1 kg/2 lb fillet salmon, skinned and visible bones removed**
> **1 tablespoon vegetable oil**
> **2 limes, each cut into 8 thin slices**
> **16 fresh dill sprigs**
> **crushed black peppercorns**
> **toasted bagel**

method

1. Preheat covered barbecue to a medium-low heat. Place smoking chips and wine in a non-reactive metal dish and soak for 20 minutes. Place dish containing smoking chips in barbecue over hot coals, cover barbecue with lid and heat for 5 minutes or until liquid is hot.
2. Cut salmon into 8 equal pieces (a) and brush with oil. Place 2 lime slices and 2 dill sprigs on each piece of salmon (b), then sprinkle with black peppercorns to taste.
3. Place salmon on oiled barbecue grill, cover barbecue with lid and smoke for 5 minutes (c). You may wish to intensify the smoke flavor by extending the cooking time according to your taste. Serve salmon on slices of toasted bagel, with Béarnaise sauce if desired.

....
Serves 8

tip from the chef

When using wood or wood products for barbecuing or smoking, always use untreated wood. Those products specifically sold for barbecuing and smoking will be free of chemicals. Hickory wood is a popular choice for smoking, but there are other woods available which impart different flavors —so experiment and find your favorite.

a

b

c

herb-infused fish

■□□ | Cooking time: 20 minutes - Preparation time: 15 minutes

method

1. Preheat barbecue to a high heat. Line one side of a large hinged fish rack with some thyme, rosemary and half the lemon slices (a).
2. Place garlic and black peppercorns in cavity of fish (b). Brush fish generously with oil and place on herbs in rack. Top with remaining lemon slices and some more rosemary and thyme. Close rack (c).
3. Place fish on barbecue and cook for 8-10 minutes each side or until flesh flakes when tested with a fork.

....
Serves 6

ingredients

> **2 bunches fresh lemon thyme sprigs**
> **1 bunch fresh rosemary sprigs**
> **2 lemons, sliced**
> **3 cloves garlic, peeled**
> **6 black peppercorns**
> **1.5 kg/3 lb whole fish such as bream, sea perch or snapper, cleaned**
> **2 tablespoons olive oil**

tip from the chef

Hinged wire racks are a useful accessory for the barbecue cook and are available in many sizes and shapes. The one used in this recipe is designed for cooking whole fish, other shapes include square or rectangular ones which are suitable for cooking burgers and fish fillets and cutlets, or any delicate food which threatens to fall apart when you try to turn it over. To prevent sticking, always oil the rack well before placing the food on it.

a

b

c

oysters
and mussels in shells

■□□ | Cooking time: 10 minutes - Preparation time: 5 minutes

method

1. Preheat barbecue to a high heat. Place mussels and oysters on barbecue grill and cook for 3-5 minutes or until mussel shells open and oysters are warm. Discard any mussels that do not open after 5 minutes cooking.

2. Place butter, parsley, lemon juice, orange juice and wine in a heavy-based saucepan, place on barbecue and cook, stirring, for 2 minutes or until mixture is bubbling. Place mussels and oysters on a serving platter, drizzle with butter mixture and serve immediately.

ingredients

> **500 g/1 lb mussels, scrubbed and beards removed**
> **24 oysters in half shells**
> **60 g/2 oz butter, softened**
> **1 tablespoon chopped fresh parsley**
> **2 tablespoons lemon juice**
> **1 tablespoon orange juice**
> **1 tablespoon white wine**

....

Serves 6

tip from the chef

Mussels will live out of water for up to 7 days if treated correctly. To keep mussels alive, place them in a bucket, cover with a wet towel and top with ice. Store in a cool place and as the ice melts, drain off the water and replace ice. It is important that the mussels do not sit in the water or they will drown.

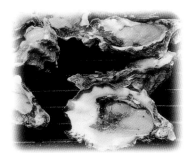

spiced
chicken sandwiches

■ ■ ☐ | Cooking time: 10 minutes - Preparation time: 20 minutes

method

1. Preheat barbecue to a medium heat.
2. To make marinade, place yogurt, coriander, curry paste, chutney and lemon juice in a shallow dish and mix to combine. Add chicken breasts, turn to coat and marinate for 20 minutes.
3. To make raita, cut cucumber in half, lengthwise and scrape out seeds. Cut cucumber into fine slices and place in a bowl. Add yogurt, garlic and lemon juice and mix to combine. Cover and chill until ready to serve.
4. Drain chicken and cook on oiled barbecue grill for 4 minutes each side or until tender and cooked through. To serve, place chicken fillets on 4 pieces of bread, then top with tomatoes and raita and remaining pieces of bread.

Makes 4 sandwiches

ingredients

> **4 boneless chicken breast fillets**
> **4 pieces Turkish (pide) bread, halved**
> **4 tomatoes, sliced**

spiced yogurt marinade

> **$1/2$ cup/100 g/$3^1/2$ oz natural yogurt**
> **4 tablespoons chopped fresh coriander**
> **2 tablespoons mild red curry paste**
> **2 tablespoons mango chutney**
> **2 tablespoons lemon juice**

cucumber raita

> **1 cucumber**
> **1 cup/200 g/$6^1/2$ oz thick natural yogurt**
> **1 clove garlic, crushed**
> **1 tablespoon lemon juice**

tip from the chef

Turkish bread (pide) is a flat white leavened bread similar to Italian flatbread. It is usually baked in ovals measuring 30-40 cm/12-16 in. If Turkish bread is unavailable, country-style Italian bread, rye bread, sour dough, ciabatta or focaccia are all good alternatives for this recipe.

quick
chicken satay

■■□ | Cooking time: 35 minutes - Preparation time: 15minutes

method

1. Place oil, soy sauce, garlic and ginger in a bowl and mix to combine. Add chicken and marinate for 15 minutes.
2. Drain chicken, thread onto lightly oiled skewers and cook on a preheated medium barbecue for 15-20 minutes or until chicken is cooked.
3. To make sauce, heat oil in a saucepan over a medium heat, add garlic and ginger and cook, stirring, for 2 minutes. Stir in stock, coconut milk and soy sauce, bring to simmering and simmer for 5 minutes.
4. Add peanut butter and simmer for 5 minutes longer. Just prior to serving, stir in chili sauce. Serve sauce with chicken.

Serves 4

ingredients

> 1 tablespoon vegetable oil
> 1 tablespoon soy sauce
> 1 large clove garlic, crushed
> 1/2 teaspoon finely grated fresh ginger
> 500 g/1 lb boneless chicken thigh or breast fillets, skinned and cut into 2.5 cm/1 in cubes

satay sauce
> 1 teaspoon vegetable oil
> 2 large cloves garlic, crushed
> 2 teaspoons finely grated fresh ginger
> 1 cup/250 ml/8 fl oz chicken stock
> 1 cup/250 ml/8 fl oz coconut milk
> 1 tablespoon soy sauce
> 2 tablespoons crunchy peanut butter
> 2 teaspoons sweet chili sauce

tip from the chef

The sauce can be made in advance and stored in a sealed container in the refrigerator for 5-7 days. Reheat over a low heat before serving. If sweet chili sauce is not available mix ordinary chili sauce with a little brown sugar.

pakistani
chicken skewers

■□□ | Cooking time: 10 minutes - Preparation time: 10 minutes

ingredients

> **1 onion, chopped**
> **2 cloves garlic, crushed**
> **1 tablespoon finely grated fresh ginger**
> **1 tablespoon mild masala paste**
> **1/2 cup/100 g/3 1/2 oz natural yogurt**
> **8 boneless chicken breast fillets, cut into 2 cm/ 3/4 in cubes**

method

1. Place onion, garlic, ginger, masala paste and yogurt into food processor or blender and process until smooth.
2. Transfer yogurt mixture to a bowl, add chicken and toss to coat. Cover and marinate for 2 hours.
3. Thread chicken onto lightly oiled skewers and cook on a lightly oiled preheated hot barbecue for 10 minutes or until chicken is tender.

Serves 6-8

tip from the chef

When using bamboo skewers, soak them in cold water for at least an hour before using them on a barbecue; this will prevent them from burning. Lightly oiling the skewers ensures that the food does not stick to them during cooking.

oriental
chicken kebabs

■ □ □ | Cooking time: 10 minutes - Preparation time: 20 minutes

method

1. Preheat barbecue to a high heat.
2. To make marinade, place sugar, lime leaves, if using, chili, soy sauce and lime juice in a bowl and mix to combine. Add chicken, toss to coat and marinate for 20 minutes. Drain chicken.
3. Thread chicken and mushrooms onto lightly oiled skewers and cook on oiled barbecue grill, turning and basting with reserved marinade, for 5 minutes or until chicken is tender and cooked.
4. Place snow pea sprouts or watercress, carrots and spring onions in a bowl. Combine sugar and lime juice, pour over salad and toss. Pile salad onto serving plates, then top with chicken kebabs.

Serves 6

ingredients

> 3 boneless chicken breast fillets, sliced
> 12 shiitake mushrooms
> 185 g/6 oz snow pea sprouts or watercress
> 2 carrots, shredded
> 4 spring onions, chopped
> 2 teaspoons sugar
> 2 tablespoons lime juice

chili and lime marinade

> 1 tablespoon brown sugar
> 3 kaffir lime leaves, shredded (optional)
> 1 fresh red chili, chopped
> 2 tablespoons soy sauce
> 1 tablespoon lime juice

tip from the chef

Try kebabs with barbecued garlic flatbread. To make it, combine 1 tablespoon olive oil and 2 cloves garlic, crushed, and lightly brush both sides of 3 pieces lavash bread or pitta bread rounds. Cook on barbecue grill for about 1-2 minutes each side or until golden. Break into pieces to serve.

greek
honey lemon chicken

■□□ | Cooking time: 20 minutes - Preparation time: 10 minutes

method

1. To make marinade, place garlic, rosemary, oregano, oil, lemon juice and honey in a ceramic or glass dish and mix to combine. Add chicken, cover and marinate at room temperature for 15 minutes.
2. Drain chicken and reserve marinade. Cook chicken, basting frequently with reserved marinade, on a preheated medium barbecue for 10 minutes each side or until cooked. Place any remaining marinade in a saucepan and heat over a low heat. Serve with chicken.

Serves 4

ingredients

> **8 boneless chicken thigh fillets or 4 boneless chicken breast fillets, skinned and all visible fat removed**

lemon honey marinade

> **5 cloves garlic, crushed**
> **2 teaspoons dried rosemary**
> **1 teaspoon dried oregano**
> **1/4 cup/60 ml/2 fl oz olive oil**
> **1/4 cup/60 ml/2 fl oz lemon juice**
> **1 tablespoon honey**

tip from the chef

For a more pronounced flavor marinate chicken in the refrigerator overnight.

lemon
spit-roasted chickens

■ ■ □ | Cooking time: 1 hour - Preparation time 15 minutes

ingredients

> **2 x 1.2 kg/2¹/₂ lb chickens**
> **1 lemon, quartered**
> **2 onions, quartered**
> **4 sprigs fresh rosemary**
> **4 cloves garlic, halved**

herb butter

> **125 g/4 oz butter, softened**
> **2 tablespoons chopped fresh rosemary**
> **2 tablespoons chopped fresh lemon thyme**

method

1. Preheat barbecue to a high heat. Wash chickens and pat dry with absorbent kitchen paper. Place 2 lemon quarters, 4 onion quarters, 2 rosemary sprigs and 4 garlic clove halves in the cavity of each chicken (a).

2. To make herb butter, place butter, chopped rosemary and thyme in a bowl and mix to combine. Using your fingers, carefully loosen the skin over the breasts of the chickens, then spread butter under it (b).

3. Thread chickens onto the spit and secure with clamps at both ends (c) to stop chickens from spinning when cooking. Place spit over barbecue and cook for 1 hour or until chickens are tender.

Serves 6-8

tip from the chef

Spit-roasting is best done on a gas barbecue with volcanic rock or charcoal. To prevent flare-ups during cooking place a tray of water in the barbecue under the chickens. This catches the fat which drips out during cooking. Check the manufacturer's instructions on how to install the spit on your barbecue.

a

b

c

grilled
lemon grass chicken

■□□ | Cooking time: 10 minutes - Preparation time: 10 minutes

method

1. To make paste, place onion, garlic, ginger, lemon grass, chili, sugar and lemon juice in a food processor or blender and process to make a rough paste.
2. Rub paste over chicken pieces, cover and marinate in the refrigerator for at least 5 hours or preferably overnight.
3. Preheat barbecue to a high heat. Cook chicken on oiled barbecue grill for 4-5 minutes each side or until tender.

....
Serves 4

ingredients

> **8 chicken pieces, approximately 1.5 kg/3 lb**

lemon grass and garlic paste

> **1 small onion, chopped**
> **2 cloves garlic, chopped**
> **2 cm/1/4 in piece fresh ginger, sliced**
> **2 stalks fresh lemon grass, chopped or 1 teaspoon dried lemon grass, soaked in hot water until soft**
> **1 fresh red chili, chopped**
> **1 tablespoon sugar**
> **2 tablespoons lemon juice**

tip from the chef

Fresh lemon grass is available from Oriental food shops and some greengrocers and supermarkets. If using dried lemon grass, soak it in hot water for 20 minutes or until soft before using. Lemon grass is also available in bottles in supermarkets. Use this in the same way as you would fresh lemon grass.

italian hamburgers

a

b

■□□ I Cooking time: 8 minutes - Preparation time: 15 minutes

method

1. To make patties, place beef, sun-dried tomatoes, parsley, basil, garlic and Worcestershire sauce in a bowl and mix to combine (a). Shape mixture into 8 mini patties (b), place on a plate lined with plastic food wrap and chill until required.
2. Preheat barbecue to a high heat. Brush eggplant slices and pepper quarters with oil (c) and cook on barbecue grill for 2 minutes each side or until tender. Place in a bowl, add vinegar and toss to combine.
3. Reduce barbecue heat to medium, then cook patties for 4 minutes each side (d) or until cooked to your liking. To assemble, spread base of rolls with pesto, then top with some rocket leaves, a patty, some slices of eggplant and a piece of red pepper and cover with top of roll. Serve immediately.

Makes 8 mini hamburgers

ingredients

> 2 small eggplant, thinly sliced
> 2 red peppers, quartered
> 2 tablespoons olive oil
> 1/3 cup/90 ml/3 fl oz balsamic vinegar
> 8 mini rosetta rolls, split
> 3 tablespoons ready-made pesto
> 125 g/4 oz rocket leaves

beef patties

> 500 g/1 lb lean beef mince
> 3 tablespoons finely chopped sun-dried tomatoes
> 2 tablespoons chopped fresh parsley
> 1 tablespoon chopped fresh basil
> 2 cloves garlic, crushed
> 1 tablespoon Worcestershire sauce

c

d

tip from the chef

Mini hamburgers are a creative alternative for a teenagers' barbecue.

oriental
pork ribs

■□□ | Cooking time: 1 hour 50 minutes - Preparation time: 20 minutes

ingredients

> **1.5 kg/3 lb pork spareribs**
> **2 cloves garlic, crushed**
> **1 tablespoon finely grated fresh ginger**
> **1 tablespoon chopped fresh coriander**
> **1 teaspoon five spice powder**
> **1/4 cup/60 ml/2 fl oz soy sauce**
> **2 tablespoons sweet chili sauce**
> **2 tablespoons hoisin sauce**
> **1 tablespoon tomato sauce**
> **1 tablespoon sherry**
> **1 teaspoon rice vinegar**

method

1. Place ribs on a wire rack set in a baking dish and bake at 180°C/350°F/Gas 4 for 1¹/₂ hours. Set aside to cool slightly.
2. Preheat barbecue to a medium heat. Place garlic, ginger, coriander, five spice powder, soy sauce, chili sauce, hoisin sauce, tomato sauce, sherry and vinegar in a bowl and mix to combine. Add ribs and toss to coat.
3. Drain ribs and reserve liquid. Place ribs on lightly oiled barbecue plate and cook, turning and basting frequently with reserved liquid, for 10 minutes or until ribs are tender.

....
Serves 6

tip from the chef
Five spice powder is a pungent, fragrant, spicy and slightly sweet powder which is a mixture of star anise, fennel, Szechwan peppercorns, cloves and cinnamon. It adds a delicate anise flavor to foods.

chili peanut ribs

■ ☐ ☐ | Cooking time: 10 minutes - Preparation time: 5 minutes

method

1. Place oil, garlic, ginger, chilies, curry paste and coconut milk in a bowl and mix to combine.
2. Place ribs in shallow glass or ceramic dish, pour over coconut milk mixture, turn to coat, cover and set aside to marinate for 2 hours.
3. Drain ribs and cook on a lightly oiled preheated hot barbecue for 5 minutes each side or until meat is tender.

....

Serves 4

ingredients

> 1 tablespoon vegetable oil
> 2 cloves garlic, crushed
> 2 tablespoons finely grated fresh ginger
> 3 small fresh red chilies, finely chopped
> 3 tablespoons satay curry paste
> 1 cup/250 ml/8 fl oz coconut milk
> 1 kg/2 lb beef spare ribs

tip from the chef

To store fresh ginger, peel and place in a glass jar. Cover with sherry or green ginger wine, store in the refrigerator and use as you would fresh ginger. Ginger will keep in this way for many months. The sherry or wine left after the ginger was used is ideal either for cooking or dressings.

herbed
and spiced pork loin

■■□ | Cooking time: 2 hours 30 minutes - Preparation time: 20 minutes

ingredients

> **2 kg/4 lb boneless pork loin, rolled and rind scored at 2 cm/³/4 in intervals**

herb and spice marinade
> **1 onion, chopped**
> **2 tablespoons crushed pink peppercorns**
> **2 tablespoons crushed green peppercorns**
> **2 tablespoons ground coriander**
> **1 tablespoon freshly ground black pepper**
> **1 tablespoon ground cumin**
> **1 teaspoon garam masala**
> **1 teaspoon ground mixed spice**
> **1 teaspoon turmeric**
> **1 teaspoon paprika**
> **1 teaspoon sea salt**
> **2 tablespoons peanut oil**
> **2 tablespoons sesame oil**
> **1 tablespoon white vinegar**

method

1. To make marinade, place onion, pink peppercorns, green peppercorns, coriander, black pepper, cumin, garam masala, mixed spice, turmeric, paprika, salt, peanut oil, sesame oil and vinegar into a food processor or blender and process to make a paste.
2. Rub marinade over pork, place in a glass or ceramic dish, cover and marinate in the refrigerator overnight.
3. Preheat a covered barbecue to a medium heat. Place pork on lightly oiled barbecue grill and cook, turning frequently, for 2-2¹/2 hours or until pork is tender and cooked through. Stand for 10 minutes before carving and serving.

···········
Serves 8

tip from the chef
When scoring the rind take care not to cut through into the flesh.

sweet
rosemary cutlets

a

■□□ | Cooking time: 10 minutes - Preparation time: 20 minutes

method

1. Make 2 slits in the thin outer covering of each cutlet and insert a rosemary sprig into each one (a). Place prepared cutlets in a shallow dish.
2. To make marinade, place wine, honey, mustard and black pepper to taste in a bowl and mix to combine (b). Pour marinade over cutlets (c), turn to coat and marinate for 40 minutes.
3. Preheat barbecue to a high heat. Drain cutlets, place on oiled barbecue grill and cook for 4-5 minutes each side (d) or until cooked to your liking.

....

Serves 6

ingredients

> **12 small double lamb cutlets (allow 2 double cutlets per serve)**
> **24 small sprigs rosemary**

honey and wine marinade

> **1 cup/250 ml/8 fl oz red wine**
> **¹/₃ cup/90 ml/3 fl oz honey**
> **2 tablespoons wholegrain mustard**
> **crushed black peppercorns**

tip from the chef

Remember always to check the barbecue area before lighting the barbecue. Do not have the barbecue too close to the house, and sweep up any dry leaves or anything that might catch fire if hit by a spark.

b

c

d

tandoori cutlets

■□□ | Cooking time: 10 minutes - Preparation time: 10 minutes

ingredients

> **2 tablespoons tandoori curry paste**
> **1 tablespoon lime juice**
> **1 tablespoon chopped fresh coriander**
> **1 teaspoon ground cumin**
> **1 teaspoon ground coriander**
> **1 teaspoon ground turmeric**
> **1 teaspoon ground cloves**
> **1¹/4 cups/250 g/8 oz natural yogurt**
> **12 lamb cutlets, trimmed of all visible fat**

yogurt mint sauce

> **¹/2 cup/100 g/3¹/2 oz natural yogurt**
> **1 clove garlic, crushed**
> **1 teaspoon ground cumin**
> **1 tablespoon finely chopped mint**

method

1. Place curry paste, lime juice, fresh coriander, cumin, ground coriander, turmeric, cloves and yogurt in a bowl and mix to combine. Place cutlets in a shallow glass or ceramic dish, spoon over yogurt mixture and turn to coat. Cover and marinate in the refrigerator overnight.

2. Drain cutlets and reserve marinade. Cook cutlets on a lightly oiled preheated hot barbecue, brushing frequently with reserved marinade, for 5 minutes each side or until tender.

3. To make sauce, place yogurt, garlic, cumin and mint in a bowl and mix to combine. Serve with cutlets.

....
Serves 6

tip from the chef

Accompany these spicy lamb cutlets with a tomato sambal. To make sambal, place 2 finely chopped tomatoes, 1 seeded and finely sliced fresh green chili, 1 tablespoon lemon juice, 1 tablespoon finely chopped onion and 1 tablespoon desiccated coconut in a bowl and mix to combine.

fresh herb chops

■□□ | Cooking time: 10 minutes - Preparation time: 10 minutes

method

1. To make marinade, place rosemary, thyme, garlic, oil, vinegar and lime juice in a shallow glass or ceramic dish and mix to combine. Add lamb, turn to coat, cover and marinate at room temperature for 1 hour.
2. Preheat barbecue to a high heat. Drain lamb, place on lightly oiled barbecue and cook for 3-5 minutes each side or until chops are cooked to your liking.

....

Serves 6

ingredients

> **12 lamb neck chops, trimmed of excess fat**

fresh herb marinade

> **2 tablespoons chopped fresh rosemary**
> **2 tablespoons chopped fresh thyme**
> **2 cloves garlic, crushed**
> **1/4 cup/60 ml/2 fl oz olive oil**
> **1/4 cup/60 ml/2 fl oz balsamic or red wine vinegar**
> **2 tablespoons lime juice**

tip from the chef

Long-handled tongs are a must for turning food without burning your hands.

barbecued
port-glazed lamb

■□□ I Cooking time: 2 hours - Preparation time: 10 minutes

ingredients
> **2.5 kg/5 lb leg of lamb**
> **1 cup/250 ml/8 fl oz port**
> **1½ cups/375 ml/12 fl oz water**

port glaze
> **4 tablespoons Dijon mustard**
> **2 teaspoons finely grated orange rind**
> **½ teaspoon grated nutmeg**
> **1½ cups/375 ml/12 fl oz port**
> **½ cup/125 ml/4 fl oz honey**
> **2 tablespoons balsamic vinegar**

method
1. Preheat covered barbecue to a medium heat.
2. To make glaze, place mustard, orange rind, nutmeg, port, honey and vinegar in a saucepan, bring to simmering over a low heat and simmer until mixture thickens and reduces slightly.
3. Place lamb on a wire rack set in a roasting tin and brush with glaze. Pour port and water into roasting tin, place on barbecue, cover with lid and cook for 2 hours, brushing with glaze at 15-minute intervals, or until cooked to your liking.

....

Serves 8

tip from the chef
Check the quantity of liquid in the roasting tin regularly during cooking and add more water if required.

grilled
apple stacks

a

■ □ □ | Cooking time: 5 minutes - Preparation time: 10 minutes

method

1. Preheat barbecue to a low heat. Cut each apple crosswise into 4 thick slices (a). Combine lemon juice and honey and brush over apple slices (b).
2. Cook apple slices on oiled barbecue grill (c) for 2 minutes each side or until golden. Transfer apples to a bowl and chill.
3. To make filling, place ricotta cheese, sugar, lemon juice and vanilla essence in a food processor or blender and process until smooth (d).
4. To serve, place an apple slice on each serving plate. Top with a spoonful of ricotta filling and another apple slice.

ingredients

> 3 apples, cored
> 2 tablespoons lemon juice
> 1 tablespoon honey

ricotta filling

> 250 g/8 oz ricotta cheese
> 2 tablespoons sugar
> 2 tablespoons lemon juice
> 1 teaspoon vanilla essence

....

Serves 6

tip from the chef

For this recipe, purchase fresh ricotta cheese in a piece. It has a smoother texture than that which comes in the small tubs. Fresh ricotta cheese is available from specialty cheese shops, delicatessens and some supermarkets.

b

c

d

grilled nectarines

■□□ I Cooking time: 5 minutes - Preparation time: 10 minutes

ingredients

> $^1/_4$ cup/60 g/2 oz caster sugar
> $^1/_3$ cup/90 ml/3 fl oz marsala or sweet sherry
> 1 tablespoon lemon juice
> 6 nectarines, stoned and quartered

vanilla mascarpone

> 100 g/3$^1/_2$ oz ricotta cheese
> 155 g/5 oz mascarpone
> 2 tablespoons sugar
> 1 teaspoon vanilla essence
> 1 tablespoon marsala or sweet sherry

method

1. Preheat barbecue to a medium heat. Place caster sugar, marsala or sherry and lemon juice in a bowl and mix to combine. Add nectarines (a) and macerate for 5 minutes.
2. Drain nectarines and reserve liquid. Place nectarines on barbecue plate and cook for 1 minute each side (b) or until golden. Return nectarines to macerating liquid (c) until ready to serve.
3. For mascarpone, place ricotta cheese, mascarpone, sugar, vanilla and marsala or sherry in a bowl (d) and beat until smooth. Serve with nectarines.

Serves 6

tip from the chef

This recipe is also delicious made with fresh peaches.

a

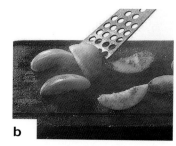

b

c

d

grilled
strawberry kebabs

■□□ | Cooking time: 1 minute - Preparation time: 5 minutes

method

1. Preheat barbecue to a high heat.
2. Thread strawberries onto lightly oiled wooden skewers. Brush strawberries with vinegar, then roll in icing sugar.
3. Cook kebabs on oiled barbecue grill for 10 seconds each side or until icing sugar caramelizes. Serve immediately with ice cream.

ingredients

> 500 g/1 lb strawberries, halved
> 1/4 cup/60 ml/2 fl oz balsamic vinegar
> 1 1/2 cups/220 g/7 oz icing sugar
> vanilla ice cream

Serves 8

tip from the chef

Remember to soak bamboo or wooden skewers in water before using –this helps to prevent them from burning during cooking. Before threading food onto skewers, lightly oil them so that the cooked food is easy to remove. For this recipe, use a light tasting oil such as canola or sunflower.

coconut
rice parcels

■□□ I Cooking time: 30 minutes - Preparation time: 15 minutes

method

1. Preheat barbecue to a medium-high heat. Place rice, water, coconut milk and sugar in a saucepan and bring to the boil over a high heat. Reduce heat and simmer for 10-15 minutes or until liquid is absorbed.
2. Place banana leaves, if using, in a shallow dish, pour over boiling water to cover and soak for 5 minutes. Drain.
3. Divide half the rice between the banana leaves or foil. Spread rice out evenly, then top with banana mixture. Cover with remaining rice, fold banana leaf or aluminum foil to enclose and secure with a wooden toothpick or cocktail stick. Cook parcels on barbecue grill for 2 minutes each side or until heated through.

ingredients

> **375 g/12 oz jasmine rice**
> **2 cups/500 ml/16 fl oz water**
> **200 ml/6$^{1}/_{2}$ fl oz coconut milk**
> **$^{1}/_{4}$ cup/60 g/2 oz sugar**
> **4 x 30 cm/12 in squares banana leaf or aluminum foil**
> **1 banana, mashed with 1 tablespoon lemon juice**

....
Serves 4

tip from the chef

These rice parcels are delicious served with coconut or vanilla ice cream. Banana leaves can be purchased from Oriental food shops and some greengrocers and supermarkets. Leaves are not eaten but they impart distinctive flavor to the rice. They can be softened by blanching as in this recipe. Alternatively, heat in a covered microwavable dish on High (100%) for 45-60 seconds or until soft. For easier wrapping, remove the thick mid-rib from the leaves.

notes

best of asia

table of contents

introduction

Have a look at a table full of Asian exotic dishes.
It will be very difficult for you to choose among
sushi subtleties, bittersweet dishes and curry
fervor. That is why this book contains dishes
representative of Thailand, China, Japan and India
as well as some of Indonesia and Malaysia.
The aim is to provide a synthetic and complete
panorama of that immense
continent to curious cooks.

best of asia
introduction

Rather than following completely authentic formulas, we have preferred to gather creative recipes based on traditional ingredients and methods which reflect a style of cooking that we are sure will appeal to you and your guests. Go ahead then and travel to Asia taking our attractive suggestions as a starting point. And do not scare at the mentioning of uncommon products. Even though their names may be unknown to you, you can get them at supermarkets or Oriental food stores. Below you will find some references about them and so will you in "tips from the chef" at the end of the recipes.

- **Cellophane noodles** are soy noodles that become transparent when hydrated.
- **Galanga** is the root of a plant belonging to the ginger family. It has a sweet flavor and a strong aroma which reminds us of cinnamon and citrus.

- **Garam masala** is a highly scented mix of cardamom, cinnamon, nutmeg, mace and cumin.
- **Kaffir lime leaves** are the highly aromatic leaves from a citrus tree native of South-Asia.
- **Kechap manis** is a thick sweet seasoning sauce made of soy sauce, sugar and spices, used in Indonesian cooking.
- **Mirin** is amber-colored sugary wine made of rice. It is only used in cooking.
- **Nori** is a kind of seaweed. It is sold in sheets which are similar to dark green cellophane.
- **Oyster sauce** is made of oysters cooked in soy sauce and brine. It is thick, dark brown and intensely aromatic.
- **Rice vinegar** is clear, sweet and fragrant.
- **Sesame oil** is made from roasted sesame seeds and has a strong flavor.
- **Shrimp paste** is a pungent ingredient made by pounding dried salted shrimp.
- **Tamarind pulp** is made from the fruit of the tamarind or Indian date tree, which is seeded and peeled and then pressed into a dark brown pulp.
- **Thai fish sauce**, also known as **nam pla**, is the drained liquid from salted fermented anchovies. It has a pungent taste.

Difficulty scale

■□□□ I Easy to do

■■□□ I Requires attention

■■■■ I Requires experience

seafood
and tofu soup

■■■ | Cooking time: 10 minutes - Preparation time: 10 minutes

ingredients

> **10 uncooked medium prawns, shelled and deveined, tails left intact**
> **125 g/4 oz squid, cleaned**
> **1/2 teaspoon salt**
> **1/2 teaspoon sugar**
> **1/2 teaspoon cornflour**
> **1/4 teaspoon freshly ground black pepper**
> **1/4 teaspoon sesame oil**
> **185 g/6 oz firm white fish fillets, sliced**
> **1 tablespoon vegetable oil**
> **3-5 thin slices fresh ginger**
> **300 g/9 1/2 oz tofu, sliced**
> **1 small carrot, sliced**
> **2 teaspoons chicken stock powder**
> **2-3 spring onions, cut into 2.5 cm/1 in lengths**

method

1. Cut prawns in half lengthwise. Make a single cut down the length of each squid tube or body and open out. Using a sharp knife, cut parallel lines down the length of the squid, taking care not to cut right through the flesh. Make more cuts in the opposite direction (a) to form a diamond pattern. Cut each piece into 3 or 4 pieces.

2. Place salt, sugar, cornflour, black pepper, sesame oil and 1 tablespoon water in a bowl and mix to combine. Add prawns, squid and fish (b), toss to combine and set aside to marinate for 10-15 minutes.

3. Heat vegetable oil in a wok or large saucepan, add ginger and stir-fry for 2-3 minutes or until fragrant. Stir in 3 cups/750 ml/1 1/4 pt water and bring to the boil. Add seafood mixture, tofu, carrot and chicken stock powder and cook for 5 minutes or until seafood is cooked. Remove pan from heat, sprinkle with spring onions (c) and serve immediately.

....
Serves 4

tip from the chef

Either fresh or frozen squid can be used for this dish. Freezing squid has no adverse effect on it –in fact more often than not it tenderizes it.

a

b

c

hot and sour
seafood soup

■□□ | Cooking time: 15 minutes - Preparation time: 10 minutes

method

1. Place shallots, chilies, lime leaves, ginger and stock in a saucepan and bring to the boil over a high heat. Reduce heat and simmer for 3 minutes.
2. Add fish, prawns, mussels and mushrooms and cook for 3-5 minutes or until fish and seafood are cooked, discard any mussels that do not open. Stir in lime juice and fish sauce.
3. To serve, ladle soup into bowls, scatter with coriander leaves and accompany with lime wedges.

....

Serves 6

ingredients

> 4 red or golden shallots, sliced
> 2 fresh green chilies, chopped
> 6 kaffir lime leaves
> 4 slices fresh ginger
> 8 cups/2 litres/3¹/₂ pt fish, chicken or vegetable stock
> 250 g/8 oz firm fish fillets, cut into chunks
> 12 medium uncooked prawns, shelled and deveined
> 12 mussels, scrubbed and beards removed
> 125 g/4 oz oyster or straw mushrooms
> 3 tablespoons lime juice
> 2 tablespoons Thai fish sauce
> fresh coriander leaves
> lime wedges

tip from the chef

Straw mushrooms are one of the most popular mushrooms used in Asian cooking and in the West are readily available canned. Oyster mushrooms are also known as abalone mushrooms and range in color from white to grey to pale pink. Their shape is similar to that of an oyster shell and they have a delicate flavor. Oyster mushrooms should not be eaten raw as some people are allergic to them in the uncooked state.

creamy corn and crab soup

■□□ | Cooking time: 8 minutes - Preparation time: 5 minutes

ingredients

> 440 g/14 oz canned creamed corn
> 1³/4 cup/440 ml/14 fl oz water
> 185 g/6 oz crabmeat
> 1¹/2 teaspoons cornflour blended with 1 tablespoon water
> 1 egg, lightly beaten
> 1 teaspoon vinegar
> ¹/4 teaspoon sugar
> freshly ground black pepper

method

1. Place corn and water in a saucepan and bring to the boil over a medium heat. Stir in crabmeat and cornflour mixture and bring to simmering.
2. Remove from heat, stir in egg, vinegar and sugar and season to taste with black pepper. Serve immediately.

Serves 4

tip from the chef

For something different make this soup using pork mince instead of the crabmeat.

chili
kumara soup

■□□ | Cooking time: 25 minutes - Preparation time: 10 minutes

method

1. Place stock, lemon grass, chilies, galanga or ginger and coriander roots in a saucepan and bring to the boil over a medium heat. Add kumara and simmer, uncovered, for 15 minutes or until soft.
2. Remove lemon grass, galanga or ginger and coriander roots and discard. Cool liquid slightly, then purée soup, in batches, in a food processor or blender.
3. Return soup to a clean saucepan and stir in $1/2$ cup/125 ml/4 fl oz of the coconut cream and the fish sauce. Cook, stirring, over a medium heat for 4 minutes or until heated. Stir in two-thirds of the reserved coriander leaves.
4. To serve, ladle soup into bowls, top with a little of the remaining coconut cream and scatter with remaining coriander leaves.

....

Serves 4

ingredients

> **6 cups/1.5 litres/ $2^1/2$ pt chicken stock**
> **3 stalks fresh lemon grass, bruised, or $1^1/2$ teaspoons dried lemon grass, soaked**
> **3 fresh red chilies, halved**
> **10 slices fresh or bottled galanga or fresh ginger**
> **5-6 fresh coriander plants, roots washed, leaves removed and reserved**
> **1 large kumara, peeled and cut into 2 cm/ $3/4$ in pieces**
> **$3/4$ cup/185 ml/6 fl oz coconut cream**
> **1 tablespoon Thai fish sauce**

tip from the chef

Coriander is used extensively in Thai cooking and it is one of the ingredients that gives Thai food its distinctive flavor. Fresh coriander is readily available from greengrocers and is usually sold as the whole plant.

avocado sushi

■■□ I Cooking time: 25 minutes - Preparation time: 20 minutes

ingredients

> **2 cups short grain rice**
> **3 cups water**
> **$1/3$ cup rice vinegar**
> **$1/3$ cup sugar**
> **3 teaspoons salt**
> **5 sheets nori**
> **2 teaspoons wasabi paste**
> **1 small green cucumber, peeled, seeded, cut into thin strips**
> **1 avocado, peeled, cut into thin strips**
> **60 g/2 oz sliced pickled ginger, cut into thin strips**

method

1. Combine rice and water in pan, bring to the boil, reduce heat, simmer, uncovered until water is absorbed. Cover pan, simmer 5 minutes.
2. Stir in combined vinegar, sugar and salt. Arrange nori sheets in single layer on oven tray. Toast in moderate oven 2 minutes or until crisp.
3. Cut a strip about 4 cm/1$1/2$ in wide from the narrow end of the nori sheet. Place the large piece of nori in the center of a bamboo mat, place the extra narrow strip in the center; this helps strengthen the nori during rolling.
4. Spread about a fifth of the rice over nori. At the end furthest away from you leave a 4 cm/1$1/2$ in edge. Make a hollow with wet fingers horizontally across the center. Spread the wasabi paste along hollow in rice. Place a combination of cucumber, avocado and ginger in hollow of rice.
5. Use bamboo mat to help roll the sushi, pressing firmly as you roll. Remove bamboo mat. Use a sharp knife to cut sushi into 4 cm/1$1/2$ in slices.

....
Serves 4

tip from the chef

Nori, wasabi paste and pickled ginger are available from Asian food shops.

tuna
and prawn sushi

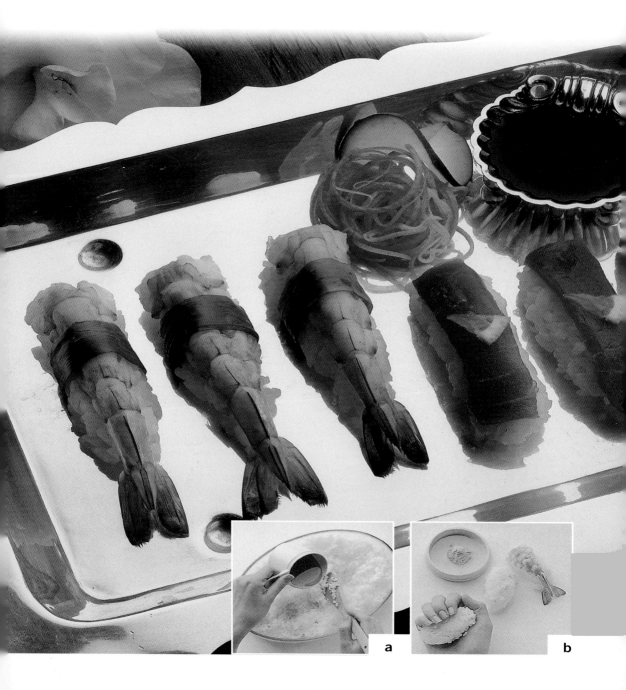

a

b

■■□ | Cooking time: 20 minutes - Preparation time: 20 minutes

method

1. To make rice, wash rice several times in cold water and set aside to drain for 30 minutes. Place rice and water in a large saucepan and bring to the boil, cover and cook, without stirring, over a low heat for 15 minutes. Remove pan from heat and set aside for 10 minutes.

2. Place mirin or sherry, vinegar, sugar and salt in a small saucepan and bring to the boil. Remove pan from heat and set aside to cool.

3. Turn rice out into a large shallow dish, pour over vinegar mixture (a) and toss gently until rice has cooled to room temperature. Take a tablespoon of rice in your hand and gently squeeze it to form a neat oval (b). Place on a serving platter and repeat with remaining rice to make 24 ovals.

4. Split prawns on the underside —taking care not to cut all the way through— and flatten them out. Mix wasabi powder with a few drops of water to make a smooth paste and dab a little on each rice oval. Top twelve rice ovals with prawns.

5. Cut tuna into twelve 2 x 4 cm/ 3/4 x 1 1/2 in strips each 5 mm/1/4 in thick. Top remaining rice ovals with tuna strips. Wrap a strip of nori, if using, around each sushi. Serve sushi with soy sauce for dipping.

Makes 24

ingredients

> 12 large cooked prawns, shelled, deveined, tails left intact
> 2 teaspoons wasabi powder
> 125 g/4 oz extremely fresh tuna
> 1 sheet nori, cut into strips (optional)
> soy sauce

sushi rice

> 500 g/1 lb short grain rice
> 2 1/2 cups/600 ml/ 1 pt water
> 2 tablespoons mirin or sherry
> 4 tablespoons rice vinegar
> 2 tablespoons sugar
> 1/2 teaspoon salt

tip from the chef

Strips of spring onion can be used in place of the nori if you wish. Wasabi is a very hot horseradish powder; it is available from Asian food stores.

vegetable
pilau

■□□ I Cooking time: 45 minutes - Preparation time: 10 minutes

ingredients

> 500 g/1 lb mixed
  vegetables such as peas,
  diced potatoes, sliced
  beans, diced zucchini,
  diced carrot and
  cauliflower flowerets
> 2 tablespoons
  vegetable oil
> 1 onion, sliced
> 1 bay leaf
> 1 cinnamon stick
> 1/2 teaspoon fennel seeds
> 1/2 teaspoon cumin seeds
> 1/2 teaspoon black
  mustard seeds
> 1/2 teaspoon yellow
  mustard seeds
> 1/4 teaspoon fenugreek
  seeds
> 2 teaspoons finely
  chopped fresh ginger
> 2 fresh red or green
  chilies, finely chopped
> 2 cups/440 g/14 oz rice
> 5 cups/1.2 litres/2 pt hot
  water
> 2 hard-boiled eggs, sliced
> 2 tomatoes, sliced
> 60 g/2 oz salted cashews,
  roughly chopped
> 90 g/3 oz sultanas

method

1. Boil, steam or microwave vegetables until partially cooked. Drain and set aside.
2. Heat oil in a large saucepan, add onion, bay leaf, cinnamon stick, fennel, cumin, mustard and fenugreek seeds, ginger and chilies and cook over a medium heat for 1 minute.
3. Stir in rice and mix well to combine. Add mixed vegetables and cook for 2 minutes. Stir in hot water and transfer rice mixture to a casserole dish. Cover and bake at 180°C/350°F/Gas 4 for 20-30 minutes or until rice is cooked.
4. Place rice mixture on a large serving platter. Decorate border with alternate slices of egg and tomato, then sprinkle with cashews and sultanas.

....

Serves 4

tip from the chef
The decorative garnish is optional, but it makes for an attractive presentation.

a

noodle
baskets with vegetables

■■□ | Cooking time: 15 minutes - Preparation time: 10 minutes

method

1. To make baskets, divide noodles into four equal portions. Use one portion of noodles to line a medium-sized metal sieve, then press another smaller metal sieve over the noodles to form a basket shape (a).
2. Heat oil in a wok over a high heat until a cube of bread dropped in browns in 50 seconds. Deep-fry noodle baskets (b) for 2 minutes or until noodles are crisp and golden. Turn basket onto absorbent kitchen paper to drain and repeat with remaining noodles to make four baskets.
3. Heat sesame oil and 1 tablespoon vegetable oil together in a clean wok over a medium heat, add spring onions, ginger and garlic and stir-fry for 2 minutes. Add carrot, red pepper and asparagus (c) and stir-fry for 3 minutes.
4. Add mushrooms, corn, soy sauce and honey and stir-fry for 2 minutes or until heated through. Spoon vegetables into noodle baskets.

ingredients

> 1 teaspoon sesame oil
> 1 tablespoon vegetable oil
> 3 spring onions, sliced
> 1 tablespoon finely grated fresh ginger
> 2 cloves garlic, crushed
> 1 carrot, sliced
> 1 red pepper, cut into thin strips
> 250 g/8 oz asparagus, cut into 5 cm/2 in lengths
> 125 g/4 oz oyster mushrooms
> 60 g/2 oz canned baby sweet corn cobs
> 1/4 cup/60 ml/2 fl oz soy sauce
> 1 tablespoon honey

noodle baskets

> 125 g/4 oz fresh thin egg noodles, cooked and drained well
> vegetable oil for deep-frying

....
Serves 4

b

c

tip from the chef

Noodle baskets can be made several hours in advance, however do not cook the vegetables and fill the baskets until immediately prior to serving.

crispy noodles with lime pickle

■□□ | Cooking time: 50 minutes - Preparation time: 15 minutes

ingredients

> 220 g/7 oz cellophane noodles
> 6 small fresh red chilies, finely sliced
> 4 red or golden shallots, finely chopped
> 30 g/1 oz fresh coriander leaves, chopped
> 30 g/1 oz fresh basil leaves, chopped
> 1 tablespoon roasted shrimp paste (optional)
> 1/4 cup/60 ml/2 fl oz peanut oil

lime pickle

> 4 limes, sliced
> 6 red or golden shallots, sliced
> 1 tablespoon salt
> 1/2 cup/125 ml/4 fl oz water
> 1/2 cup/90 g/3 oz brown sugar
> 1/4 cup/60 ml/2 fl oz vinegar
> 1 tablespoon Thai fish sauce
> 1 tablespoon black mustard seeds

method

1. To make pickle, place limes, shallots, salt and water in a saucepan and cook, stirring occasionally, over a medium heat for 10-15 minutes or until limes are tender. Stir in sugar (a), vinegar, fish sauce and mustard seeds and simmer, stirring frequently, for 30 minutes or until pickle is thick.

2. Place noodles in a bowl, pour over boiling water (b) to cover and stand for 10 minutes or until soft. Drain well. Add chilies, shallots, coriander, basil and shrimp paste (if using) to noodles and mix well.

3. Heat oil in a large frying pan over a medium heat, place small handfuls of noodle mixture in pan, shape into a rough round and flatten with a spatula (c). Cook for 3-4 minutes each side or until golden and crisp. Drain on absorbent kitchen paper and serve with pickle.

....

Serves 6

tip from the chef

When making the pickle take care not to let it catch on the bottom of the pan. The pickle can be made in advance and stored in the refrigerator or if keeping for more than 2 weeks seal in a sterilized jar.

a

b

c

noodle
vegetable rolls

■□□ | Cooking time: 0 minute - Preparation time: 15 minutes

method

1. Dip a rice paper round into cold water, then place on a clean tea-towel, to absorb any excess moisture.
2. To assemble, place a little of the cucumber, carrot, sprouts, noodles, mint, basil, coriander and peanuts along the center of each rice paper round leaving a 2 cm/ 3/4 in border. Place a chive (if using) across the center so that the end with the flower hangs over one edge.
3. To roll, fold up one edge of rice paper over filling to form base of roll, then roll up to enclose filling. Repeat with remaining rice paper rounds, filling and chives. Serve immediately with chili sauce for dipping.

....
Makes 12

ingredients

> 12 large rice paper rounds
> sweet chili sauce

noodle vegetable filling

> 2 cucumbers, seeded and cut into 5 cm/ 2 in strips
> 2 carrots, cut into 5 cm/2 in strips
> 60 g/2 oz bean sprouts
> 60 g/2 oz rice vermicelli noodles, cooked and drained well
> 30 g/1 oz fresh mint leaves
> 30 g/1 oz fresh basil leaves
> 15 g/1/2 oz fresh coriander leaves
> 4 tablespoons chopped roasted peanuts
> 12 garlic chives with flower (optional)

tip from the chef

Traditionally the garlic chive pops out the open end of the roll as a garnish. Oriental rice paper is made from a paste of ground rice and water which is stamped into rounds and dried. When moistened the brittle sheets become flexible. It is used to make delicacies such as these rolls. Sold in sealed packets rice paper can be purchased from Oriental food stores.

baked fish

◼️◻️◻️ | Cooking time: 25 minutes - Preparation time: 15 minutes

ingredients

> 2 large onions, roughly chopped
> 1 tablespoon vegetable oil
> 2 cloves garlic, crushed
> 2 fresh red or green chilies, finely chopped
> 2 teaspoons finely chopped fresh ginger
> 1 tablespoon cumin seeds
> 2 bay leaves
> 4 large tomatoes, finely chopped
> 1/2 teaspoon mango powder
> 1/2 teaspoon ground cumin
> 1/2 teaspoon ground coriander
> 1/4 teaspoon ground turmeric
> pinch ground cloves
> pinch ground cinnamon
> pinch ground cardamom
> 3 tablespoons cream
> 4 firm white fish fillets
> 1 bunch fresh basil, leaves removed and finely chopped

method

1. Place onions in a food processor or blender and process to make a purée (a). Heat oil in a heavy-based saucepan, add garlic, chilies, ginger, cumin seeds, bay leaves and onion purée and cook over a medium heat until onions are a pinkish color. Add tomatoes (b), mango powder and spices and cook, stirring, for 3-4 minutes. Remove pan from heat and stir in cream.

2. Place fish in a baking dish, pour over sauce (c) and bake at 180°C/350°F/Gas 4 for 20 minutes or until fish flakes when tested with a fork. Just prior to serving, sprinkle with basil.

....
Serves 4

tip from the chef

Fresh herb raita is the perfect accompaniment to fish. To make raita, place 1 cup natural yogurt and 1/4 cup water in a bowl and whip until smooth. Coarsely chop 1/4 bunch coriander, 3 sprigs mint, 3 sprigs basil, 3 sprigs dill and 12 chives and add to yogurt mixture, mix to combine.

a

b

c

deep-fried
chili fish

■■□ I Cooking time: 15 minutes - Preparation time: 15 minutes

method

1. Make diagonal slashes along both sides of the fish.
2. Place chopped chilies, coriander roots, garlic and black peppercorns in a food processor and process to make a paste. Spread mixture over both sides of fish and marinate for 30 minutes.
3. To make sauce, place sugar, sliced chilies, shallots, vinegar and water in a saucepan and cook, stirring, over a low heat until sugar dissolves. Bring mixture to simmering and simmer, stirring occasionally, for 4 minutes or until sauce thickens.
4. Heat vegetable oil in a wok or deep-frying pan until a cube of bread dropped in browns in 50 seconds. Cook fish, one at a time, for 2 minutes each side or until crisp and flesh flakes when tested with a fork. Drain on absorbent kitchen paper. Serve with chili sauce.

Serves 6

ingredients

> 2 x 500 g/1 1b lean whole fish (bream, whiting or cod)
> 4 fresh red chilies, chopped
> 4 fresh coriander roots
> 3 cloves garlic, crushed
> 1 teaspoon crushed black peppercorns
> vegetable oil for deep-frying

red chili sauce

> 2/3 cup/170 g/5 1/2 oz sugar
> 8 fresh red chilies, sliced
> 4 red or golden shallots, sliced
> 1/3 cup/90 ml/3 fl oz coconut vinegar
> 1/3 cup/90 ml/3 fl oz water

tip from the chef

This dish is a stunning centerpiece for a Thai feast.

stuffed
calamari rings

■■□ | Cooking time: 40 minutes - Preparation time: 20 minutes

ingredients

> **4 lettuce leaves**
> **4 large squid, cleaned, tentacles chopped**
> **4 sheets nori**
> **1/2 cup/125 ml/4 fl oz light soy sauce**
> **1/2 cup/125 ml/4 fl oz water**
> **3 tablespoons sugar**

method

1. Place lettuce leaves in a bowl, cover with boiling water, then drain.
2. Place one-quarter of the squid tentacles on a lettuce leaf, wrap up tightly (a) then enclose in a nori sheet and seal by lightly wetting the edge. Repeat with remaining tentacles, lettuce leaves and nori sheets.
3. Insert tentacle parcels in squid hoods (b) and secure ends with a wooden toothpick.
4. Place soy sauce, water and sugar in a saucepan, bring to simmering, then add squid and simmer for 30-40 minutes or until tender. Using a slotted spoon remove squid, drain and refrigerate overnight. To serve, cut into slices.

Makes 36 slices

tip from the chef

As a general guide, allow 250 g/8 oz of raw squid per serving when making quick-cooking dishes such as stir-fries and allow 500 g/1 lb per serving when braising or stewing. On longer cooking you will find that considerable shrinkage takes place, hence the larger quantity required.

a

b

stir-fried
tamarind prawns

■□□ | Cooking time: 8 minutes - Preparation time: 15 minutes

method

1. Place tamarind pulp and water in a bowl and stand for 20 minutes. Strain, reserve liquid and set aside. Discard solids.
2. Heat oil in a wok or frying pan over a high heat, add lemon grass or rind and chilies and stir-fry for 1 minute. Add prawns and stir-fry for 2 minutes or until they change color.
3. Add mangoes, coriander, sugar, lime juice and tamarind liquid and stir-fry for 5 minutes or until prawns are cooked.

....

Serves 4

ingredients

> 2 tablespoons tamarind pulp
> 1/2 cup/125 ml/4 fl oz water
> 2 teaspoons vegetable oil
> 3 stalks fresh lemon grass, chopped, or 2 teaspoons finely grated lemon rind
> 2 fresh red chilies, chopped
> 500 g/1 lb medium uncooked prawns, shelled and deveined, tails left intact
> 2 green (unripe) mangoes, peeled and thinly sliced
> 3 tablespoons chopped fresh coriander leaves
> 2 tablespoons brown sugar
> 2 tablespoons lime juice

tip from the chef

Lemon grass is an aromatic herb, native of India. It is widely used in Thai and Vietnamese cooking.

shellfish
with lemon grass

■■☐☐ | Cooking time: 10 minutes - Preparation time: 15 minutes

method

1. Place shallots, lemon grass, garlic, ginger, chilies and lime leaves in a small bowl and mix to combine.
2. Place mussels in a wok and sprinkle over half the shallot mixture. Pour in water, cover and cook over a high heat for 5 minutes.
3. Add scallops, remaining shallot mixture, lime juice, fish sauce and basil and toss to combine. Cover and cook for 4-5 minutes or until mussels and scallops are cooked. Discard any mussels that do not open.

....

Serves 4

ingredients

> **5 red or golden shallots, chopped**
> **4 stalks fresh lemon grass, bruised and cut into 3 cm/1 1/4 in pieces, or 2 teaspoons dried lemon grass, soaked**
> **3 cloves garlic, chopped**
> **5 cm/2 in piece fresh ginger, shredded**
> **3 fresh red chilies, seeded and chopped**
> **8 kaffir lime leaves, torn into pieces**
> **750 g/1 1/2 lb mussels, scrubbed and beards removed**
> **1/4 cup/60 ml/2 fl oz water**
> **12 scallops on shells, cleaned**
> **1 tablespoon lime juice**
> **1 tablespoon Thai fish sauce**
> **3 tablespoons fresh basil leaves**

tip from the chef

Serve this dish at the table straight from the wok and don't forget to give each diner some of the delicious cooking juices.

mussels
with coconut vinegar

■ □ □ | Cooking time: 10 minutes - Preparation time: 10 minutes

method

1. Place mussels, coriander, lemon grass, ginger and water in a wok over a high heat. Cover and cook for 5 minutes or until mussels open. Discard any mussels that do not open. Remove mussels from wok, discard coriander, lemon grass and ginger. Strain cooking liquid and reserve.

2. Heat oil in a wok over a medium heat, add onion and chilies and stir-fry for 3 minutes or until onion is soft. Add mussels, reserved cooking liquid and coconut vinegar and stir-fry for 2 minutes or until mussels are heated. Scatter with coriander leaves and serve.

....
Serves 4

ingredients

> **1.5 kg/3 lb mussels, scrubbed and beards removed**
> **6 whole coriander plants, washed and roughly chopped**
> **3 stalks fresh lemon grass, bruised, or 1 1/2 teaspoons dried lemon grass, soaked**
> **5 cm/2 in piece fresh ginger, shredded**
> **1/2 cup/125 ml/4 fl oz water**
> **1 tablespoon vegetable oil**
> **1 red onion, halved and sliced**
> **2 fresh red chilies, sliced**
> **2 tablespoons coconut vinegar**
> **fresh coriander leaves**

tip from the chef

This dish is delicious served with boiled egg noodles and topped with coriander leaves and wok juices.
Coconut vinegar is made from the sap of the coconut palm. It is available from Oriental food shops. If unavailable any mild vinegar can be used instead.

chicken
in oyster sauce

■□□ | Cooking time: 10 minutes - Preparation time: 10 minutes

ingredients

> 2¹/2 tablespoons vegetable oil
> 500 g/1 lb chicken pieces, chopped into bite-sized pieces
> 4 fresh green chilies, cut into 1 cm/¹/2 in pieces
> 3 thin slices fresh ginger
> ¹/3 cup/90 ml/3 fl oz oyster sauce
> 1 teaspoon dark soy sauce
> ¹/2 teaspoon sugar
> ¹/2 teaspoon salt
> 2 cloves garlic, sliced
> 2 spring onions, sliced diagonally
> 2 tablespoons chopped fresh coriander

method

1. Heat oil in a wok or frying pan over a high heat. Add chicken, chilies and ginger and stir-fry for 3-4 minutes or until chicken is golden.
2. Stir in oyster sauce, soy sauce, sugar, salt and garlic and stir-fry for 3-4 minutes longer or until chicken is cooked. Sprinkle with spring onions and coriander and serve immediately.

....
Serves 4

tip from the chef

When handling fresh chilies do not put your hands near your eyes or allow them to touch your lips. To avoid discomfort and burning, wear rubber gloves. Freshly minced chili is available in jars from supermarkets.

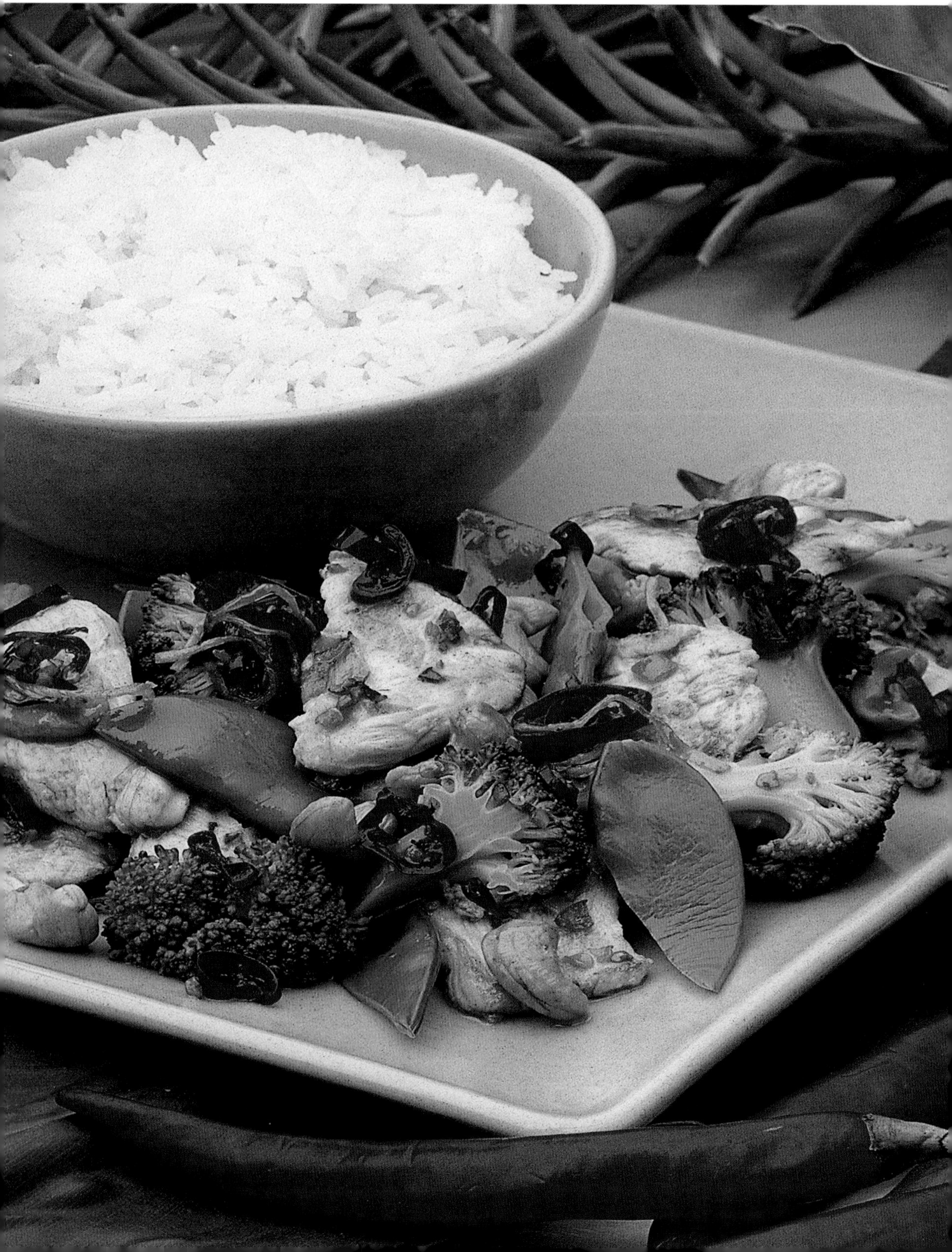

chicken
with chili jam

■ □ □ I Cooking time: 12 minutes - Preparation time: 10 minutes

method

1. To make jam, heat oil in a wok over a medium heat, add chilies, ginger and shrimp paste and stir-fry for 1 minute or until golden. Stir in sugar, water and lime juice and cook, stirring, for 3 minutes or until mixture is thick. Remove jam from wok and set aside.
2. Heat oil in a clean wok over a high heat for 1 minute, add chicken and shallots and stir-fry for 3 minutes or until lightly browned.
3. Add broccoli, snow peas, cashews and soy sauce and stir-fry for 3 minutes longer or until vegetables change color and are cooked.
4. To serve, place chicken on serving plate and top with chili jam.

....
Serves 4

ingredients

> 2 teaspoons vegetable oil
> 3 boneless chicken breast fillets, cut into thin strips
> 4 red or golden shallots, chopped
> 185 g/6 oz broccoli, chopped
> 125 g/4 oz snow peas, halved
> 60 g/2 oz unsalted roasted cashews
> 2 tablespoons soy sauce

chili jam

> 2 teaspoons vegetable oil
> 4 fresh red chilies, sliced
> 1 tablespoon shredded fresh ginger
> 1 teaspoon shrimp paste
> 1/3 cup/90 g/3 oz sugar
> 1/3 cup/90 ml/3 fl oz water
> 2 tablespoons lime juice

tip from the chef

Serve this tasty chicken dish with steamed jasmine rice. If you prefer, the chili jam can be served separately so that each diner can season their serving according to individual taste.

charcoal-grilled
chicken

■□□ I Cooking time: 30 minutes - Preparation time: 15 minutes

ingredients

> **1 kg/2 lb chicken pieces**
> **4 fresh red chilies, chopped**
> **4 cloves garlic, chopped**
> **3 fresh coriander roots, chopped**
> **2 stalks fresh lemon grass, chopped, or 1 teaspoon dried lemon grass, soaked**
> **3 tablespoons lime juice**
> **2 tablespoons soy sauce**
> **1 cup/250 ml/8 fl oz coconut cream**
> **sweet chili sauce**

method

1. Place chicken in a ceramic or glass dish and set aside.
2. Place chilies, garlic, coriander roots, lemon grass, lime juice and soy sauce in a food processor and process to make paste. Mix paste with coconut cream and pour over chicken. Marinate for 1 hour.
3. Drain chicken and reserve marinade. Cook chicken over a slow charcoal or gas barbecue or under a preheated low grill, brushing frequently with reserved marinade, for 25-30 minutes or until chicken is tender. Serve with chili sauce.

....

Serves 6

tip from the chef

Fresh lemon grass is available from Oriental food shops and some supermarkets and greengrocers. It is also available dried; if using dried lemon grass soak it in hot water for 20 minutes or until soft before using.

savory pancakes

a

■□□ | Cooking time: 15 minutes - Preparation time: 10 minutes

method

1. To make pancakes, whisk all ingredients (a) until smooth. Heat a lightly greased wok over a high heat, pour 2 tablespoons batter and swirl wok so batter covers base thinly and evenly. Cook for 1-2 minutes or until bubbles form on the surface, turn (b) and cook until golden. Remove from wok and keep warm. Repeat with remaining batter.
2. To make filling, soak mushrooms in boiling water for 10 minutes or until tender. Drain, remove stalks and dice mushrooms. Heat oil in a wok over a medium heat, stir-fry onion for 2-3 minutes. Add mince and stir-fry for 2-3 minutes or until it changes color. Stir in carrot, mushrooms, soy sauce, salt, sesame oil, sugar and black pepper and cook for 4-5 minutes longer. Add potato (c) and coriander, mix. Remove from heat, cool.
3. Divide filling between pancakes, fold in sides and roll up. Serve hot or warm.

....
Makes 8

ingredients

pancakes

> **1 cup/125 g/4 oz flour**
> **$1/4$ teaspoon salt**
> **pinch sugar**
> **1 cup/250 ml/8 fl oz water**
> **1 egg**
> **1 teaspoon vegetable oil**

meat and vegetable filling

> **3 dried Chinese mushrooms, diced**
> **1 tablespoon vegetable oil**
> **1 small onion, diced**
> **125 g/4 oz mince of your choice**
> **1 small carrot, diced**
> **1 teaspoon light soy sauce**
> **$1/2$ teaspoon salt**
> **$1/2$ teaspoon sesame oil**
> **$1/2$ teaspoon sugar**
> **pinch black pepper**
> **2 large potatoes, cooked and mashed**
> **2 tablespoons chopped fresh coriander**

b

c

tip from the chef

This dish can be made ahead of time and reheated in the microwave on High (100%) for 2 minutes.

bean sprouts and pork stir-fry

■□□ | Cooking time: 8 minutes - Preparation time: 10 minutes

ingredients

> **4 dried Chinese mushrooms**
> **1 teaspoon oyster sauce**
> **sugar**
> **1 teaspoon soy sauce**
> **1/4 teaspoon salt**
> **1/4 teaspoon sesame oil**
> **pinch sugar**
> **pinch freshly ground black pepper**
> **185 g/6 oz lean pork, cut into thin strips**
> **2 tablespoons vegetable oil**
> **2.5 cm/1 in piece fresh ginger, cut into thin strips**
> **250 g/8 oz bean sprouts**
> **2 spring onions, cut into 5 cm/2 in strips**
> **1/2 red pepper, cut into thin strips**
> **2 cloves garlic, sliced**
> **1/2 teaspoon cornflour blended with 11/2 tablespoons water and 1/4 teaspoon sesame oil**

method

1. Place mushrooms in a bowl, cover with boiling water and soak for 10 minutes or until mushrooms are tender. Drain, remove stalks and cut mushrooms into strips. Place mushrooms in a small bowl, add oyster sauce and 1/4 teaspoon sugar, toss to coat and set aside.
2. Place soy sauce, salt, sesame oil, sugar and black pepper in a bowl and mix to combine. Add pork, toss to combine and marinate for 10-15 minutes.
3. Heat 1 tablespoon vegetable oil in a wok or frying pan over a medium heat, add pork mixture, mushrooms and ginger and stir-fry for 2-3 minutes or until pork changes color. Remove pork mixture from pan and set aside.
4. Heat remaining vegetable oil in pan over a medium heat, add bean sprouts, spring onions, red pepper and garlic and stir-fry for 1 minute. Return pork mixture to pan and stir in cornflour mixture. Cook, stirring, for 1 minute or until mixture thickens slightly and is heated through.

Serves 4

tip from the chef

Chinese mushrooms are pretty expensive, but you will need only a few to give this dish a special touch.

spicy mince stir-fry

■□□ | Cooking time: 8 minutes - Preparation time: 10 minutes

method

1. Heat oil in a wok or frying pan over a high heat, add onion and chilies and stir-fry for 2-3 minutes or until fragrant.
2. Add garlic, beef, mushrooms, peas, light soy sauce, Worcestershire sauce, cornflour mixture, kechap manis, sugar, salt and black pepper and stir-fry for 5 minutes or until mixture is almost dry.
3. Remove pan from heat, stir in coriander and serve immediately.

Serves 4

ingredients

> 1 1/2 tablespoons vegetable oil
> 1 onion, chopped
> 2 fresh red chilies, chopped
> 1 clove garlic, chopped
> 500 g/1 lb lean beef mince
> 2 mushrooms, chopped
> 125 g/4 oz fresh or frozen peas
> 1 1/2 tablespoons soy sauce
> 1 1/2 tablespoons Worcestershire sauce
> 1 teaspoon cornflour blended with 1 tablespoon water
> 1/2 teaspoon kechap manis
> 1 teaspoon sugar
> 3/4 teaspoon salt
> 1/4 teaspoon freshly ground black pepper
> 1 tablespoon chopped fresh coriander

tip from the chef

This mixture is delicious served in lettuce cups. Spoon the mixture into the lettuce leaves, roll up and eat.
If kechap manis is unavailable a mixture of soy sauce and golden syrup can be used in its place.

sweet
and sour pork

■□□ | Cooking time: 15 minutes - Preparation time: 15 minutes

ingredients

> 1/2 teaspoon salt
> 1/2 teaspoon sugar
> 1/4 teaspoon freshly ground pepper
> 3/4 teaspoon light soy sauce
> 1 egg yolk
> 375 g/12 oz diced lean pork
> cornflour
> oil for deep-frying

sweet and sour sauce

> 1 tablespoon vegetable oil
> 1/2 cup/125 ml/4 fl oz water
> 2 teaspoons white vinegar
> 1/2 teaspoon sesame oil
> 1/4 teaspoon salt
> 3 tablespoons sugar
> 2 1/2 tablespoons tomato sauce
> 2 teaspoons chili sauce
> 2 teaspoons Worcestershire sauce
> 1 tablespoon cornflour blended with 2 1/2 tablespoons water
> 1 onion, cut into eighths and separated
> 1 tomato, cut into eighths
> 1 cucumber, cut into chunks
> 125 g/4 oz pineapple pieces
> 1/2 red pepper, seeded and finely chopped

method

1. Combine salt, sugar, pepper, soy sauce and egg yolk. Add pork and toss to coat. Drain pork, toss in cornflour (a). Heat oil in a wok, cook pork in batches (b) for 5 minutes or until golden. Remove and drain on absorbent kitchen paper. Keep warm.

2. To make sauce, heat oil in a wok, stir in water, vinegar, sesame oil, seasonings and sauces. Bring to simmering, stirring. Add cornflour mixture and cook, stirring, for 3-4 minutes or until sauce boils and thickens. Add remaining ingredients (c) and cook, stirring, for 1 minute. Add pork and cook for 1-2 minutes longer or until heated through.

....
Serves 4

tip from the chef

This famous dish is delicious served with boiled rice and steamed Chinese cabbage.

a

b

c

barbecued
pork spare ribs

■□□ I Cooking time: 15 minutes - Preparation time: 10 minutes

method

1. Place garlic, ginger, sugar, cumin and soy sauce in a glass or ceramic bowl and mix to combine. Add spare ribs, turn to coat and marinate for 1 hour.

2. Drain ribs and reserve marinade. Cook ribs over a preheated hot barbecue or under a hot grill, basting frequently with marinade, for 15 minutes or until pork is cooked through and skin crackles.

ingredients

> **4 cloves garlic, chopped**
> **2 tablespoons finely grated fresh ginger**
> **2 tablespoons sugar**
> **2 teaspoons ground cumin**
> **$1/2$ cup dark soy sauce**
> **1 kg/2 lb pork spare ribs**

Serves 6

tip from the chef

For an informal meal, serve these tasty spare ribs with a salad of Asian greens and herbs and bowls of steamed jasmine rice.

lamb
kofta in cream sauce

■□□ | Cooking time: 50 minutes - Preparation time: 15 minutes

ingredients

lamb kofta

> 1 kg/2 lb lamb mince
> 2 tablespoons cream
> 2 teaspoons finely chopped fresh ginger
> 2 fresh chilies, finely chopped
> 3 cloves garlic, finely chopped
> 1 teaspoon mango powder
> 1 1/2 teaspoons each ground coriander, cumin and garam masala

cream sauce

> 1 tablespoon vegetable oil
> 2 bay leaves
> 2 teaspoons finely chopped fresh ginger
> 2 fresh chilies, finely chopped
> 3 cloves garlic, finely chopped
> 1 teaspoon each cumin seeds, mango powder, ground coriander, turmeric and garam masala
> 300 ml/9 1/2 fl oz cream
> 1 bunch fresh coriander, leaves chopped

method

1. To make kofta, combine all ingredients. Using wet hands, mold mixture into oval rissoles (a) and place in a steamer. Place steamer over a saucepan of boiling water (b), cover and steam for 15-20 minutes or until kofta is just cooked. Remove kofta from steamer and place in a shallow ovenproof dish. Set aside.

2. To make sauce, heat oil in a saucepan over a low heat, add spices and cook for 2 minutes. Stir in cream and cook, stirring, for 5-7 minutes. Remove from heat and stir in coriander. Spoon over kofta (c), cover and bake at 150°C/300°F/Gas 2 for 20 minutes.

Serves 6

tip from the chef

If you wish to offer spicy rice as a side dish for this tasty meatballs, wrap 1/4 teaspoon each black peppercorns, black mustard seeds and cumin seeds, 2 dried red chilies, 1 cinnamon stick, 2 cardamom pods, 2 teaspoons chopped fresh ginger and 2 bay leaves in a piece of muslin, tie securely. Place 5 cups/1.2 litres/2 pt water in a saucepan and bring to the boil. Stir in 2 cups/440 g/ 14 oz rice, 1 teaspoon lemon juice and spice bag and bring back to the boil, then reduce heat to low, cover and simmer for 12-15 minutes or until rice is cooked.

a

b

c

mogul lamb

■ ■ □ | Cooking time: 135 minutes - Preparation time: 15 minutes

method

1. Melt butter in a large saucepan, add tomatoes, chilies, ginger and garlic and cook over a medium heat, stirring frequently, for 15 minutes or until tomatoes are soft and pulpy.
2. Place black pepper, cardamom, cloves, fennel, cinnamon, fenugreek and water in a bowl and mix to combine. Stir spice mixture into tomato mixture, then add coriander, mint, basil and dill. Remove sauce from heat.
3. Place lamb in a glass or ceramic baking dish, pour over sauce, cover and marinate in the refrigerator for 15-20 hours.
4. Remove cover from baking dish and bake lamb at 180°C/350°F/Gas 4 for 2 hours or until cooked to your liking.

....

Serves 6

ingredients

> **15 g/ 1/2 oz butter**
> **750 g/1 1/2 lb ripe tomatoes, finely chopped**
> **2-3 fresh red or green chilies, finely chopped**
> **2 teaspoons finely chopped fresh ginger**
> **4 cloves garlic, finely chopped**
> **1 teaspoon freshly ground black pepper**
> **1/2 teaspoon each ground cardamom, cloves, fennel, cinnamon and fenugreek**
> **1/2 cup/125 ml/4 fl oz water**
> **2 bunches fresh coriander, leaves chopped**
> **1/2 bunch fresh mint, leaves chopped**
> **1/4 bunch fresh basil, leaves chopped**
> **1/4 bunch fresh dill, chopped**
> **1 x 1.5 kg/3 lb leg of lamb**

tip from the chef

A quicker version of this dish uses 1 kg/2 lb diced lamb, rather than a leg. Heat butter in a saucepan with chilies, ginger and garlic. Add diced lamb and cook over a low heat for 30-40 minutes. Add black pepper, cardamom, cloves, fennel, cinnamon and fenugreek and cook for 10 minutes. Stir in tomatoes and cook for 20-30 minutes or until lamb is tender. Add coriander, basil, mint and dill and cook for 5 minutes longer.

rose-flavored
dessert

■□□ | Cooking time: 10 minutes - Preparation time: 10 minutes

ingredients

gulabs

> 1 cup/75 g/2¹/2 oz skim milk powder
> ¹/3 cup/45 g/1¹/2 oz self-raising flour
> 15 g/ ¹/2 oz ghee (clarified butter)
> 100 ml/3¹/2 fl oz cream
> vegetable oil for deep-frying

syrup

> 7 cups/1.6 litres/ 3 pt water
> 3 cups/750 g/1¹/2 lb sugar
> ¹/2 teaspoon ground cardamom
> 2 teaspoons rosewater

method

1. To make syrup, place water, sugar, cardamom and rosewater in a large saucepan, cover and bring to a slow boil over a low heat.
2. To make gulabs, place milk powder, flour and ghee in a food processor and process to combine. With machine running, add enough cream to form a moist dough. Roll dough into 2 cm/3/4 in balls.
3. Heat oil in a wok until a ball dropped in sizzles slowly. Reduce heat, add remaining gulabs and cook, stirring gently, until gulabs rise to the surface. Using a slotted spoon, turn them constantly until dark golden brown.
4. Increase heat under syrup. Remove gulabs from oil and add to boiling syrup. Reduce heat and cook for 2-3 minutes or until gulabs expand and become soft. Remove pan from heat. Serve gulabs warm or at room temperature with ice cream or whipped cream if desired.

Makes about 20

tip from the chef

When cooking gulabs in the oil they must be rolled constantly and cooked quickly to prevent them from drying out and cracking. When cooking gulabs in the syrup take care not to overcook or they will become too soft and will break.

fruit salad
with almond jelly

■□□ | Cooking time: 8 minutes - Preparation time: 10 minutes

method

1. Place agar-agar powder, sugar and a little water in a bowl and mix to dissolve. Place remaining water in a saucepan and bring to the boil over a medium heat. Lower heat, stir in agar-agar mixture and cook, stirring constantly, for 5 minutes.

2. Remove pan from heat, stir in almond essence and evaporated milk and mix well to combine. Pour mixture into a shallow 20 cm/8 in square cake tin and refrigerate until set.

3. To serve, place fruit salad and lychees with juice in a large bowl. Cut jelly into bite-sized cubes and add to fruit mixture. Chill until ready to serve.

Serves 10-12

ingredients

> **2¹/₂ teaspoons agar-agar powder**
> **¹/₄ cup/60 g/2 oz caster sugar**
> **2 cups/500 ml/16 fl oz water**
> **¹/₂ teaspoon almond essence**
> **75 ml/2¹/₂ fl oz evaporated milk**
> **440 g/14 oz canned fruit salad**
> **440 g/14 oz canned lychees**

tip from the chef

Agar-agar is an extract of seaweed and is used by vegetarians instead of gelatin.

semolina
cream

■□□ | Cooking time: 40 minutes - Preparation time: 15 minutes

ingredients

> **30 g/1 oz ghee (clarified butter)**
> **2 cups/400 g/12^1/$_2$ oz fine semolina**
> **1 tablespoon sultanas**
> **1 tablespoon unsalted pistachios**
> **^{1}/$_2$ cup/125 ml/4 fl oz milk**

syrup

> **2 cups/500 ml/16 fl oz water**
> **2 cups/500 g/1 lb sugar**
> **1 tablespoon cardamom seeds**
> **pinch yellow food-coloring powder**

method

1. To make syrup, place water, sugar, cardamom seeds and food-coloring powder in a large saucepan and bring to the boil over a medium heat. Strain syrup, set aside and keep warm.
2. Melt ghee in heavy-based saucepan, stir in semolina and cook over a low heat, stirring constantly, for 20-30 minutes or until semolina changes color slightly. Take care not to burn semolina
3. Stir sultanas and pistachios into semolina mixture and cook for 3 minutes. Stir in syrup and milk and cook over a low heat, stirring constantly, for 3 minutes or until mixture thickens. Allow to cool and pour into serving glasses.

Serves 6

tip from the chef
Semolina cream is delicious served with whipped cream or ice cream.

notes

Chef
express

light & easy
desserts

table of contents

introduction

There are a lot of us who think that a meal without dessert is not complete. We share that opinion, but are aware that those delights that gratify us so much can provide undesired calories and generate reproaches from the body for not staying in shape, if these are not properly selected. Furthermore, we know that,

light and easy desserts
introduction

while the palate demands its sweet quota at the end of the menu, the stomach asks us not to overload it, as it already has quite a lot of work with the savory dishes.
How to conciliate so many opposite desires? With the exquisite dessert selection we present in this book. There are unmissable findings as they could be qualified as light both for their consistency and their relatively reduced caloric value.

- Fresh fruit is the irreplaceable basis. They provide not only color and flavor, but also necessary vitamins for a good nutrition. During the past decades, the tropical and exotic fruit availability has revolutioned the art of dessert making. In the big supermarkets, pineapple, papaya and mango are not rarities anymore, and in the gourmet boutiques you can easily find chirimoyas and star fruits.

- It is not indispensable to eliminate egg yolks, cream, or butter completely, but it is important to use them moderately.

- Thanks to the industry development, dairy products are not forbidden anymore. Light cream and low-fat yogurt are good allies that provide smoothness and greasiness. Nonfat sour cream is ideal for ice-cream, and low-fat unsalted cream cheese or cottage cheese can be used in place of ricotta cheese.

- Egg whites, rich in proteins, enable you to create airy textures. Gelatin, which has practically no calories, provides firmness to the molded desserts. Both contribute to reduce the fat content in the mixtures.

- Spices corroborate that a pinch makes the difference. Vanilla, cinnamon, anise, saffron, nutmeg, cloves and ginger rivalize against mint and citrus grated rind broadening the variety of tastes.

- Nuts add their crunchy note and wine, champagne, liqueurs and brandy show water is not the only liquid one may turn to. Even the most unconventional ingredients, such as pumpkin and tea, are main characters of this book's recipes.

Difficulty scale

■ □ □ I Easy to do

■ ■ □ I Requires attention

■ ■ ■ I Requires experience

drunken
summer fruits

■□□ I Cooking time: 0 minute - Preparation time: 10 minutes

ingredients

> 375 g/12¹/₂ oz mixed
  berries (raspberries,
  blueberries, strawberries)
> 2 white peaches,
  quartered
> 2 nectarines, quartered
> ³/₄ cup/185 ml/6 fl oz
  dessert wine
> 2 tablespoons lime juice

method

1. Place berries, peaches and nectarines in a bowl.
2. Pour wine and lime juice over fruit and toss gently to combine. Cover and chill for 20-30 minutes.
3. Serve in deep bowls with some of the marinade.

Serves 4-6

tip from the chef
When available, fresh apricots are a tasty addition to this summer dessert.

cream-topped fruit

■□□ I Cooking time: 5 minutes - Preparation time: 10 minutes

method

1. Place sugar in a saucepan. Pour just enough water over sugar to cover. Boil until it forms a golden caramel; do not stir.
2. Meanwhile, arrange fruit on a serving bowl. Top with cream and pour caramel over the top just before serving.

....

Serves 4

ingredients

> 1 cup caster sugar
> 3 tablespoons water
> 1 cup papaya, peeled, seeded and cut into 2 cm/3/4 in cubes
> 4 kiwi fruits, peeled and cut into 2 cm/3/4 in cubes
> 1/2 cup strawberries, hulled
> 4 tablespoons whipped cream

tip from the chef

Raspberry coulis is a colorful alternative to caramel. To make coulis, blend or process fresh raspberries with a little icing sugar and a dash lemon juice, then push through a sieve to discard seeds.

lychee and rockmelon salad

■□□ I Cooking time: 0 minute - Preparation time: 10 minutes

ingredients

> **1 rockmelon**
> **2 cups canned lychees, drained**
> **2 tablespoons freshly chopped mint**
> **3/4 cup sweet white wine**

method

1. Peel and seed rockmelon, cut flesh into cubes.
2. In a large bowl combine rockmelon, lychees and mint.
3. Pour over wine, toss well and refrigerate until ready to serve.

Serves 8

tip from the chef

Lychees are a rare subtropical fruit originating in South China. There the lychee is very important in their culture and is famed as "the king of fruit".

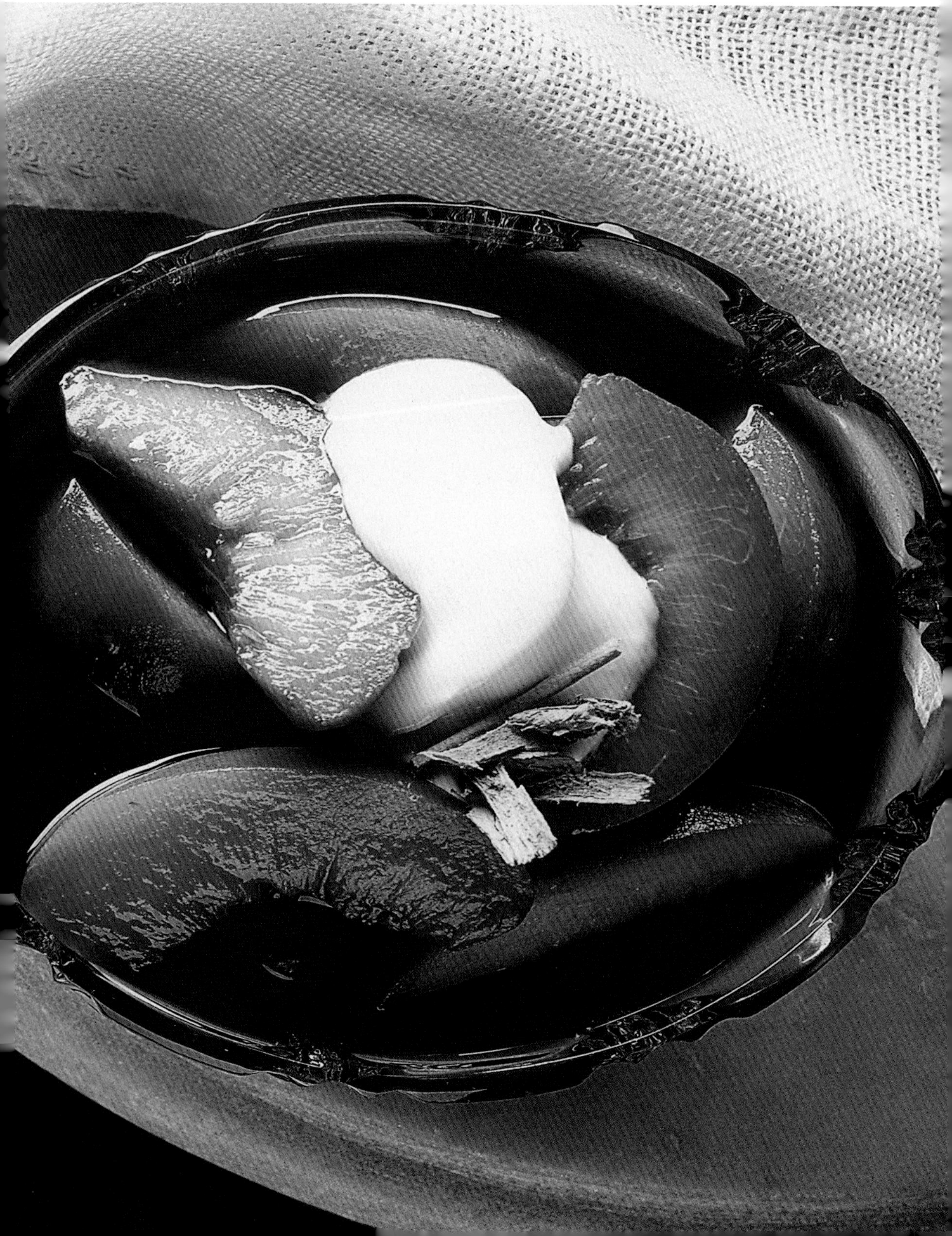

wine
compote

■□□ | Cooking time: 15 minutes - Preparation time: 10 minutes

method

1. Cut peaches into thick slices.
2. Place wine, honey and cinnamon stick into a saucepan and bring to the boil, reduce heat and simmer for 5 minutes.
3. Add peaches to saucepan and cook for 5-10 minutes or until slightly softened. Set aside to cool, then chill.

ingredients

- > **6 firm ripe peaches, halved and stones removed**
- > **1 cup/250 ml/8 fl oz red wine**
- > **2-3 tablespoons honey**
- > **1 cinnamon stick**

Serves 4

tip from the chef

As a serving suggestion, accompany with natural yogurt.

saffron-poached
pears

■□□ | Cooking time: 25 minutes - Preparation time: 10 minutes

ingredients
> **3/4 cup/185 g/6 oz sugar**
> **2 cinnamon sticks**
> **2 star anise**
> **1/4 teaspoon saffron threads**
> **8 cups/2 liters/3 1/2 pt water**
> **8 pears, peeled**

method
1. Combine sugar, cinnamon sticks, star anise, saffron and water in a large saucepan. Add pears, place over a low heat and bring to simmering. Simmer for 25 minutes or until pears are soft. Remove pan from heat and stand for 30 minutes.
2. To serve, place pears in shallow dessert bowls and spoon over poaching liquid.

Serves 8

tip from the chef
Serve this pretty dessert with thin sweet biscuits or almond bread. It can be prepared up to 3 hours in advance, however, the flavor will be best if it is not refrigerated prior to serving.

italian
stuffed peaches

■□□ | Cooking time: 25 minutes - Preparation time: 15 minutes

method

1. Cut peaches in half, peel and stone them (a).
2. In a small bowl, combine almonds, macaroons, sugar and butter, mix well (b).
3. Fill each of the peach halves with almond macaroon topping and place in a well greased baking tray (c).
4. Bake peaches in a moderate oven for 25 minutes.

....
Serves 6

ingredients

> **6 large slip-stone peaches**
> **¹/₄ cup blanched almonds**
> **¹/₂ cup crumbled macaroons**
> **3 tablespoons caster sugar**
> **4 tablespoons melted butter**

tip from the chef

These are also great for the barbecue. Wrap each filled peach half in aluminum foil and grill for 25 minutes. Serve warm.

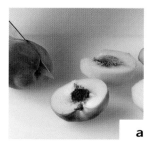

a

b

c

apricots
with pear purée

■□□ | Cooking time: 10 minutes - Preparation time: 15 minutes

ingredients

> **12 firm apricots, peeled**
> **1/2 cup/120 g/4 oz caster sugar**
> **1 teaspoon ground cinnamon**
> **1 teaspoon ground nutmeg**
> **1/2 teaspoon ground cloves**
> **1 1/2 cups canned pear halves, drained and chopped**
> **2 tablespoons freshly squeezed lemon juice**
> **2 tablespoons freshly squeezed orange juice**
> **1 tablespoon finely chopped fresh mint**
> **cinnamon sticks, to decorate**

method

1. Place peeled apricots in a saucepan with enough water to cover. Add sugar, cinnamon, nutmeg and cloves (a), simmer until tender, about 10 minutes. Cool in syrup.
2. Blend or process pears with lemon and orange juice until smooth (b), stir in mint (c).
3. Spoon some pear purée into the bottom of each plate, arrange the poached apricots in each plate on the purée and decorate with the cinnamon sticks.

Serves 4

tip from the chef

Spices are the magic touch for this simple dessert. You may like to try ginger instead of cloves.

a

b

c

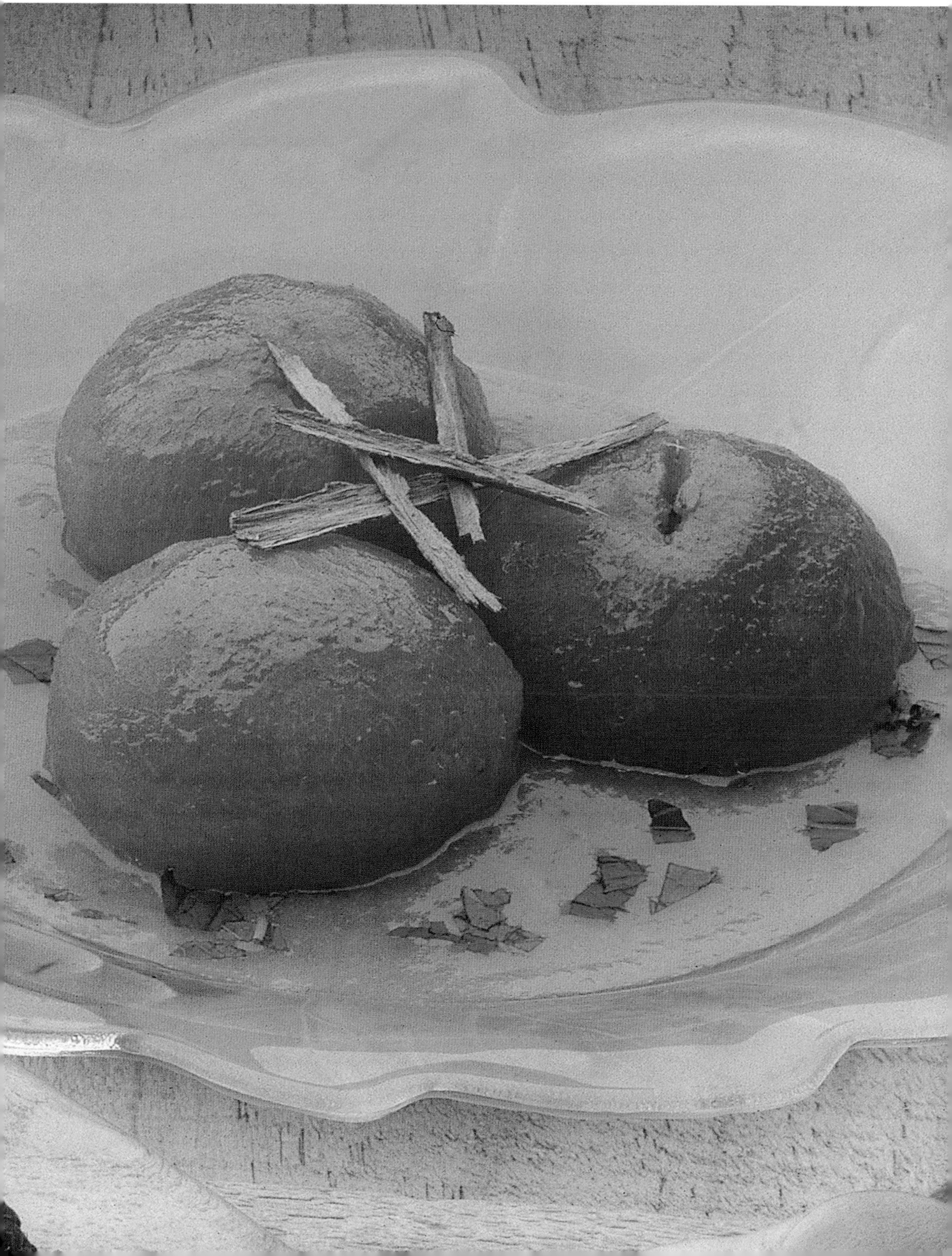

peaches
with custard

■ ■ □ | Cooking time: 35 minutes - Preparation time: 20 minutes

method

1. Place peach halves cut side down in an ovenproof dish. Evenly pour over Amaretto, sprinkle sugar over the top and bake in a moderate oven for 30 minutes.
2. Heat berries with brown sugar and 2 tablespoons water in a medium saucepan until simmering. Remove from heat, push through a sieve and discard any pips or skin. Chill purée.
3. Mix custard, cream and brandy together until combined. Spoon a puddle of custard into the base of each serving plate. Using a teaspoon, drop small dots of purée, 2 cm/³/₄ in apart, around the edge of custard. Run a skewer through the center of each dot, pulling continuously through the custard until all the dots are shaped into hearts.
4. Place two baked peach halves in the center of each custard puddle, spoon a little of the Amaretto syrup over peaches and decorate with mint.

ingredients

> **4 peaches, halved, stoned and peeled**
> **³/₄ cup/185 ml/6 fl oz Amaretto liqueur**
> **¹/₂ cup/120 g/4 oz caster sugar**
> **1 cup berries (blackberries, raspberries, blueberries)**
> **3 tablespoons brown sugar**
> **1 cup/250 ml/8 fl oz carton custard**
> **¹/₂ cup/125 ml/4 fl oz light cream**
> **2 teaspoons brandy**
> **mint to garnish**

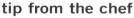

Serves 4

tip from the chef

Cointreau or another orange flavored liqueur can be used instead of Amaretto.

summer
puddings

■■□ | Cooking time: 5 minutes - Preparation time: 25 minutes

ingredients

> ¹/2 cup/120 g/4 oz caster sugar
> 2 cups/500 ml/16 fl oz water
> 875 g/1³/4 lb mixed berries (raspberries, strawberries, blueberries, blackberries)
> 14 slices bread, crusts removed

berry sauce

> 155 g/5 oz mixed berries
> 2 tablespoons icing sugar
> 1 tablespoon fresh lemon juice
> 2 tablespoons water

tip from the chef

Fresh or frozen berries can be used to make this dessert. Garnish with additional berries.

method

1. Place sugar and water in a saucepan and cook over a low heat, stirring, until sugar dissolves. Bring to the boil, reduce heat, add berries and simmer for 4-5 minutes or until fruit is soft, but still retains its shape. Drain, reserving liquid (a), and cool.
2. Cut 8 circles of bread (b). Line the base of four ¹/2 cup/125 ml/4 fl oz capacity ramekins with 4 of the bread circles. Cut remaining bread slices into fingers and line the sides of ramekins. Spoon fruit into ramekins (c) and pour enough reserved liquid to moisten bread well, then cover with remaining bread circles. Reserve any remaining liquid. Cover ramekins with aluminum foil, top with a weight, and refrigerate overnight.
3. To make sauce, process berries, icing sugar, lemon juice and water until puréed. Push mixture through a sieve to remove seeds and chill until required.
4. Turn puddings onto individual serving plates, spoon sauce over or pass separately.

....
Serves 4

a

b

c

a

b

sugar-crusted
fruit baskets

■■■ | Cooking time: 25 minutes - Preparation time: 30 minutes

method

1. To make baskets, cut each pastry sheet crosswise into 8 cm/3¹/₂ in wide strips (a). Grease outsides of 4 small, round-based ramekins and place upside down on a greased baking tray. Brush pastry strips with butter and lay over ramekins, overlapping each strip, and bringing ends down to lay flat on tray (b). Brush again with butter and sprinkle generously with sugar. Bake at 200°C/400°F/Gas 6 for 10-15 minutes or until baskets are crisp and golden.

2. To poach fruit, place sugar, water and wine in a saucepan and cook over a low heat, stirring, until sugar dissolves. Add apricots, peaches, plums and nectarines to syrup and simmer for 3-4 minutes or until fruit is just soft. Remove saucepan from heat, stir in strawberries and set aside to stand for 5 minutes. Drain.

3. To make cream, push raspberry purée through a sieve to remove seeds. Place cream in a bowl, fold in icing sugar and purée.

4. Just prior to serving, place baskets on individual serving plates, fill with fruits and top with raspberry cream.

....
Serves 6

ingredients

sugar-crusted baskets
> 6 sheets filo pastry
> 60 g/2 oz butter, melted
> ¹/₂ cup/120 g/4 oz sugar

poached fruit
> 1 cup/250 g/8 oz sugar
> 1 cup/250 ml/8 fl oz water
> ¹/₂ cup/125 ml/4 fl oz white wine
> 4 apricots, stoned and quartered
> 4 peaches, stoned and cut into eighths
> 4 plums, stoned and quartered
> 4 nectarines, stoned and cut into eighths
> 16 strawberries

raspberry cream
> 125 g/4 oz raspberries, puréed
> ³/₄ cup/185 ml/6 fl oz cream
> 4 teaspoons icing sugar

tip from the chef

Baskets are ideal for entertaining as each part can be made ahead of time. Leave the final assembly until just before serving or the fruit will cause the baskets to go soggy.

rhubarb fool

■■□ | Cooking time: 20 minutes - Preparation time: 20 minutes

ingredients

> **750 g/1¹/2 lb rhubarb, trimmed and cut into 1 cm/¹/2 in pieces**
> **1 cup/250 g/8 oz brown sugar**
> **¹/4 teaspoon ground cloves**
> **¹/2 teaspoon vanilla essence**
> **2 tablespoons lemon juice**
> **2 tablespoons orange juice**
> **¹/2 cup/100 g/3¹/2 oz cream**
> **³/4 cup/185 ml/6 fl oz natural yogurt**

method

1. Place rhubarb, sugar, cloves, vanilla essence and lemon and orange juices in a saucepan. Bring to the boil, then reduce heat and simmer, stirring occasionally, for 15 minutes or until rhubarb is soft and mixture thick. Spoon rhubarb mixture into a bowl, cover and chill.
2. Place cream in a bowl and beat until soft peaks form. Fold yogurt into cream, then fold in chilled rhubarb mixture to give a marbled effect. Spoon into individual serving glasses and chill.

Serves 8

tip from the chef

If you want to serve homemade orange biscuits with this refreshing dessert, beat 75 g/2¹/2 oz butter and 60 g/2 oz sugar until creamy, add 1 egg and 2 teaspoons grated orange rind and 90 g/3 oz flour and mix well. Place teaspoons of mixture on a baking tray and bake for 10 minutes or until golden.

pumpkin
mousse

■ ■ □ | Cooking time: 0 minute - Preparation time: 20 minutes

method

1. Sprinkle gelatin over cold water and soften for 5 minutes. Add boiling water and mix well. Stir in cream, sugar, nutmeg, vanilla and ginger. Add lemon juice and pumpkin purée, mix until well combined. Refrigerate mixture for 10-15 minutes.

2. Beat egg whites with extra sugar until soft peaks form. Whisk pumpkin mixture for 10 seconds and fold in egg whites. Spoon into serving glasses, refrigerate before serving.

....

Serves 4-6

ingredients

> **3 teaspoons gelatin**
> **4 tablespoons cold water**
> **4 tablespoons boiling water**
> **1/2 cup/125 ml/4 fl oz light cream**
> **1/4 cup/60 g/2 oz caster sugar**
> **1/2 teaspoon ground nutmeg**
> **2 teaspoons vanilla essence**
> **1 teaspoons ground ginger**
> **2 tablespoons freshly squeezed lemon juice**
> **1 cup pumpkin, cooked and puréed**
> **4 egg whites**
> **1 teaspoon caster sugar, extra**

tip from the chef

Garnish with chocolate shavings and dust with icing sugar.

colorful
glasses

■□□ I Cooking time: 5 minutes - Preparation time: 20 minutes

ingredients

> $^1/_3$ cup/90 ml/3 fl oz white wine
> 1 tablespoon lime juice
> $^1/_4$ cup/60 g/2 oz sugar
> 1$^1/_4$ cups/310 ml/10 fl oz light cream
> $^1/_3$ cup/90 ml/3 fl oz mango purée
> 250 g/8 oz strawberries, hulled and sliced
> 2 kiwi fruits, peeled and chopped
> 1 mango, peeled and thinly sliced

method

1. Place wine, lime juice and sugar in a saucepan and cook over a medium heat, stirring constantly, until sugar dissolves. Remove from heat and set aside to cool. Refrigerate until chilled.
2. Place cream, mango purée and wine mixture in a large mixing bowl and beat until soft peaks form.
3. Arrange a layer of mango slices in the base of 4 dessert glasses and top with a spoonful of mango cream. Continue layering using kiwi fruits, strawberries and mango cream, finishing with mango cream. Refrigerate until required.

Serves 6

tip from the chef
Transparent glasses are ideal to serve layered desserts like this one, as the different colors of fruit and cream look very attractive.

fig trifle

■■□ | Cooking time: 5 minutes - Preparation time: 20 minutes

method

1. Cut sponge into small cubes, blend or process until crumbled. Sprinkle with Amaretto and set aside.
2. Combine caster sugar, water, Cassis and redcurrant jelly in a small saucepan over moderate heat. Bring to the boil, reduce heat and simmer for 3 minutes.
3. Place fig slices into a bowl, pour over redcurrant syrup and set aside to cool.
4. Arrange fig slices in the bottom of 4 dessert glasses, pour over a little syrup. Combine custard and cream, pour over figs. Top with soaked crumbs, chill before serving.

Serves 4

ingredients

> 1 packed sponge cake
> 2 tablespoons Amaretto liqueur
> 1 cup/250 g/8 oz caster sugar
> 1 cup/250 ml/8 fl oz water
> 2 tablespoons Cassis liqueur
> 3 tablespoons redcurrant jelly
> 10 fresh figs, sliced
> 1 cup carton custard
> 3/4 cup/185 ml/6 fl oz light cream

tip from the chef

Both Amaretto and Cassis liqueurs enhance the flavor of this smart easy dessert.

ricotta
custard

■□□ I Cooking time: 0 minute - Preparation time: 15 minutes

ingredients
> **4 sponge finger biscuits**
> **1/4 cup/60 ml/2 fl oz Amaretto liqueur**
> **4 eggs**
> **1/2 cup/120 g/4 oz caster sugar**
> **200 g/6 1/2 oz ricotta cheese**
> **2 teaspoons vanilla essence**
> **1/4 cup/40 g/1 1/4 oz icing sugar**

method
1. Place a sponge finger biscuit in each serving glass. Drizzle Amaretto over each biscuit.
2. Beat eggs with caster sugar until light and fluffy. Blend or process ricotta cheese with vanilla essence and icing sugar until smooth. Spoon ricotta mixture into egg mixture and beat until well combined.
3. Divide custard between the serving glasses and chill for 30 minutes before serving.

....
Serves 4

tip from the chef
You can sprinkle a few toasted almonds over the top of custard to add a crunchy touch.

passion
fruit bavarois

■■□ | Cooking time: 10 minutes - Preparation time: 15 minutes

ingredients

> 1/4 cup/60 g/2 oz caster sugar
> 2 tablespoons Marsala or dry sherry
> 2 egg yolks
> 2 teaspoons gelatin
> 1 tablespoon boiling water
> 1 egg white
> 1/4 cup/60 ml/2 fl oz cream, whipped
> 1/4 cup/60 ml/2 fl oz passion fruit pulp

method

1. Place sugar, Marsala or sherry and egg yolks in a heatproof bowl set over a saucepan of simmering water. Cook, beating, for 8 minutes or until mixture is thick and leaves a ribbon trail when beaters are lifted from the mixture.
2. Dissolve gelatin in boiling water. Whisk gelatin mixture into custard mixture and set aside to cool.
3. Place egg white in a separate bowl and beat until stiff peaks form. Fold egg white mixture, cream and passion fruit pulp into custard.
4. Spoon mixture into 8 oiled small molds and refrigerate for 3 hours or until set. Unmold and garnish with extra passion fruit pulp.

....

Serves 8

tip from the chef
This dessert can be made the day before and stored, covered, in the refrigerator.

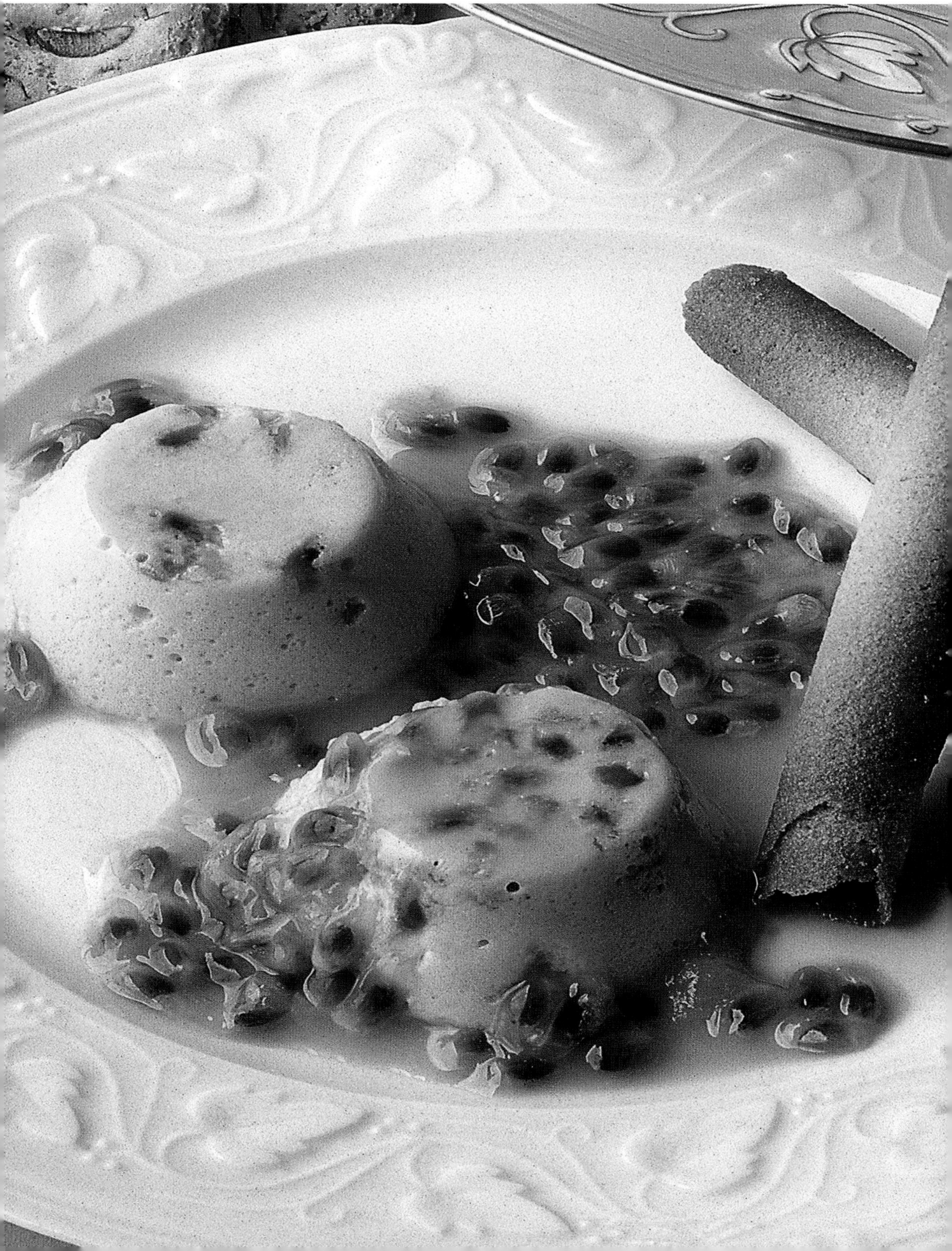

strawberry *timbales*

■□□ | Cooking time: 5 minutes - Preparation time: 15 minutes

method

1. Sprinkle gelatin over water in a cup and allow to soften for 5 minutes. Blend or process strawberries (reserving 2 for garnish) until smooth. Push purée through a sieve and pour into a small saucepan.
2. Stir in sugar and softened gelatin (a), cook purée over moderate heat for 3 minutes, stirring constantly. Transfer to a bowl.
3. Add yogurt and lime juice, mix well (b). Pour mixture into 4 fluted timbale molds (c) and refrigerate until set.
4. Beat cream with almond essence and icing sugar until just thickened. Ease timbales onto serving plates and serve with almond cream. Garnish with reserved strawberries and blanched almonds.

ingredients

> **3 teaspoons gelatin**
> **2 tablespoons water**
> **155 g/5 oz strawberries, hulled**
> **1/4 cup/60 g/2 oz caster sugar**
> **1 cup natural yogurt**
> **1 1/2 tablespoons freshly squeezed lime juice**
> **1/2 cup/125 ml/4 fl oz cream**
> **1 tablespoon almond essence**
> **1 tablespoon icing sugar**

....

Serves 4

tip from the chef

Moistening the interior part of the molds with water before filling with the mixture helps to unmold the timbales more easily.

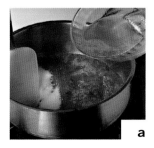
a

b

c

coconut and
lime bavarois

■□□ | Cooking time: 8 minutes - Preparation time: 5 minutes

ingredients

> **2 cups/500 ml/16 fl oz light cream**
> **3/4 cup/125 g/4 oz icing sugar**
> **1 cup/250 ml/8 fl oz coconut milk**
> **3 teaspoons gelatin**
> **1/4 cup/60 ml/2 fl oz hot water**
> **1 tablespoon lime juice**
> **toasted coconut**

method

1. Place cream and icing sugar in a saucepan over a medium heat and bring to the boil. Cool slightly, then stir in coconut milk.
2. Sprinkle gelatin over hot water, stir to dissolve and cool to the same temperature as the cream mixture. Stir gelatin mixture and lime juice into cream mixture.
3. Divide mixture between six 3/4 cup/185 ml/ 6 fl oz capacity ramekins and chill for 3-4 hours or until set. Just prior to serving, turn out and sprinkle with toasted coconut.

....

Serves 6

tip from the chef
Coconut can be quickly and easily toasted in the microwave. Simply place 1/2 cup/ 45 g/1 1/2 oz desiccated coconut on a microwavable ceramic or glass plate and cook on High (100%) for 1 minute, stir, then continue cooking and stirring at 30-60 second intervals until coconut is evenly golden. The time it takes to toast coconut in this way depends on the moisture content of the coconut – watch carefully and check frequently as the coconut can burn quickly.

apricot mold

■□□ | Cooking time: 2 minutes - Preparation time: 10 minutes

method

1. Blend or process apricots until quite smooth.
2. Dissolve gelatin in apricot nectar in a heatproof bowl over a saucepan of simmering water. Stir into apricot purée.
3. Whip cream until thick and fold into apricot mixture.
4. Pour into four lightly oiled 1/2-cup capacity molds and refrigerate until set. Serve with fresh apricot slices, whipped cream and pistachios.

ingredients

> **8 apricots, stoned and chopped**
> **3 teaspoons gelatin**
> **1/4 cup/60 ml/2 fl oz apricot nectar**
> **1 cup/250 ml/8 fl oz cream**
> **2 apricots, extra, to decorate**
> **cream to serve**
> **1/4 cup pistachios to serve**

....
Serves 4

tip from the chef

This dessert becomes even lighter if unsalted low-fat cream cheese is used in place of cream.

ricotta hearts
with coulis

■ ■ □ | Cooking time: 5 minutes - Preparation time: 20 minutes

ingredients

> 1/3 **cup cream cheese**
> 1/2 **cup natural yogurt**
> 1 **cup ricotta cheese**
> 2 **tablespoons vanilla
  essence**
> 2 **egg whites**
> 1/4 **cup/40 g/1 1/4 oz icing
  sugar**
> 1 1/4 **cups redcurrants
  or raspberries**
> 1/4 **cup water**
> 1/4 **cup/60 g/2 oz caster
  sugar**

method

1. Blend or process cream cheese with yogurt, ricotta cheese and vanilla until smooth.
2. Beat egg whites until fluffy. Gradually add icing sugar while motor is operating, beat until mixture is thick and glossy. Fold egg mixture into cheese mixture.
3. Lightly grease four 1/2-cup capacity heart-shaped molds. Carefully line with damp muslin. Spoon in mixture, make sure to fill all corners. Place in a tray and refrigerate for 4 hours until set.
4. Place redcurrants or raspberries in a small saucepan over moderate heat, add water and caster sugar, bring to the boil, reduce heat and simmer for 3 minutes. Push mixture through a sieve and chill coulis until ready to serve.
5. Turn out molds, remove muslin and pour a little coulis over mold.

....
Serves 4

tip from the chef
Garnish with some extra redcurrants if desired.

tea bavarois
with berries

■■☐ | Cooking time: 15 minutes - Preparation time: 20 minutes

method

1. Place tea and milk in a medium saucepan over moderate heat and bring to just below boiling point. Beat egg yolks and sugar together with an electric mixer until thick and creamy.

2. Remove milk and tea mixture from heat and slowly strain into egg mixture while motor is running; discard tea leaves. Return mixture to saucepan and stir constantly over a low heat until custard thickens.

3. Dissolve gelatin in hot water, whisk into custard mixture and set aside to cool to room temperature, stirring occasionally. Whip cream until fluffy and fold into cold custard.

4. Lightly oil six 1/2-cup capacity bavarois molds; pour mixture to the top, cover and refrigerate until ready to serve. To serve, turn out bavarois on dessert plates. Serve with blueberries.

ingredients

> **4 tablespoons breakfast tea**
> **2 cups/500 ml/16 fl oz milk**
> **6 egg yolks**
> **100 g/3 1/2 oz caster sugar**
> **3 teaspoons gelatin**
> **1/4 cup/60 ml/2 fl oz very hot water**
> **3/4 cup/185 ml/6 oz light cream**
> **2 cups blueberries**

....
Serves 6

tip from the chef

Decorate with icing sugar and a sprig of fresh mint.

chilled passion fruit soufflé

■ ■ □ | Cooking time: 10 minutes - Preparation time: 15 minutes

ingredients

> **4 tablespoons cornflour**
> **3 cups/750 ml/1¹/₄ pt milk**
> **¹/₂ cup/120 g/4 oz caster sugar**
> **2 teaspoons vanilla essence**
> **3 teaspoons gelatin**
> **5 tablespoons cold water**
> **¹/₂ cup/125ml/4 fl oz cream**
> **170 g/5¹/₂ oz canned passion fruit pulp**
> **¹/₂ cup toasted coconut**

method

1. In a small bowl, mix cornflour with 3 tablespoonfuls of the milk to form a paste. In a medium saucepan over moderate heat, slowly bring remaining milk, sugar, vanilla essence and cornflour paste to the boil, stirring constantly until mixture thickens. Remove from heat and cool to room temperature.
2. Dissolve gelatin in cold water, over a saucepan of simmering water, until clear. Whisk gelatin, cream and passion fruit pulp into the cooled custard and refrigerate for 10 minutes or until mixture is just beginning to set.
3. Grease four 1-cup capacity soufflé dishes and make a collar out of foil, extending 3 cm/1¹/₄ in above the height of each soufflé dish. Pour mixture into prepared dishes, enough to rise 1cm/ ¹/₂ in above the dish rim.
4. Refrigerate soufflés for 2-3 hours or until set. To serve, remove the collars and gently turn the soufflés on their side and roll the exposed edge in coconut.

....
Serves 4

tip from the chef

The passion fruit is native of tropical America and was noted by the Europeans in Brazil in the 1500's.

ruby grapefruit sorbet

■□□ | Cooking time: 5 minutes - Preparation time: 10 minutes

method

1. Place sugar, grapefruit rind and 1 cup/250 ml/8 fl oz juice in a non-reactive saucepan and cook, stirring, over a low heat until sugar dissolves.
2. Combine sugar syrup, wine and remaining juice, pour into an ice cream maker and freeze following manufacturer's instructions.
3. Alternately, pour mixture into a shallow freezerproof container and freeze until ice crystals start to form around the edges. Using a fork, stir to break up ice crystals. Repeat the process once more then freeze until firm.

ingredients

> **1 cup/250 g/8 oz sugar**
> **1 tablespoon finely grated ruby grapefruit rind**
> **4 cups/1 liter/1³/4 pt ruby grapefruit juice**
> **¹/2 cup/125 ml/4 fl oz champagne or sparkling wine**

....
Serves 8

tip from the chef

Serve sorbet in scoops with slices of peach or nectarine.

watermelon
sorbet

■□□ | Cooking time: 15 minutes - Preparation time: 10 minutes

ingredients

> ²/3 cup/170 g/5¹/2 oz
  sugar
> 1¹/4 cups/300 ml/
  10 fl oz water
> 2¹/2 cups/625 ml/1¹/4 pt
  watermelon purée
> 2 egg whites

method

1. Place sugar and water in a saucepan and cook over a low heat, stirring, until sugar dissolves. Bring to the boil, reduce heat and simmer for 10 minutes. Remove from heat and set aside to cool.
2. Mix watermelon purée into sugar syrup, pour into a freezerproof container and freeze until almost solid.
3. Place in a food processor or blender and process until smooth. Beat egg whites until soft peaks form and fold into fruit mixture. Return to freezerproof container and freeze until solid.

Makes 1.2 liters/2 pt

tip from the chef
Try these tempting variations.
Mango and passion fruit sorbet: Replace watermelon purée with 2 cups/500 ml/16 fl oz of mango purée and pulp of 4 passion fruit.
Kiwifruit sorbet: Replace watermelon purée with 2 cups/500 ml/16 fl oz of kiwifruit purée, ¹/4 cup/60 ml/2 fl oz freshly squeezed grapefruit juice and 2 tablespoons mint liqueur.

blueberry
champagne sorbet

■□□ I Cooking time: 15 minutes - Preparation time: 10 minutes

method

1. Combine sugar, champagne and water in a large saucepan over moderate heat. Bring to the boil, reduce heat and simmer for 10 minutes.
2. Blend or process blueberries with lemon juice until smooth. Add syrup (a), mix well; cool to room temperature.
3. Pour into a lamington tin, cover with foil and freeze for several hours or until partially set. Remove from freezer and break up any ice with a fork (b).
4. Beat egg whites with an electric mixer until soft peaks form, fold into blueberry ice (c) until combined. Return to freezer and serve when frozen.

....
Serves 8

ingredients

> **1¹/₂ cups/360 g/12 oz caster sugar**
> **1 cup/250 ml/8 fl oz champagne**
> **2 cups water**
> **2 small boxes blueberries**
> **¹/₂ cup/120 ml/4 fl oz freshly squeezed lemon juice**
> **2 egg whites**

tip from the chef

If using an ice-cream maker, process according to instructions.

a

b

c

pumpkin and pecan ice-cream

■□□ I Cooking time: 0 minute - Preparation time: 15 minutes

ingredients

> **8 egg yolks**
> **3/4 cup/185 g/6 oz caster sugar**
> **1 1/2 cups cooked, mashed pumpkin**
> **1 1/2 cups light cream, whipped**
> **3 teaspoons vanilla essence**
> **1 teaspoon ground cinnamon**
> **1/2 teaspoon ground nutmeg**
> **1 cup chopped pecan nuts**

method

1. Beat egg yolks with sugar until thick, pale and creamy. Fold in mashed pumpkin, whipped cream, vanilla essence, cinnamon and nutmeg.
2. Pour mixture into a loaf tin, cover with foil and freeze until partially set.
3. Remove from freezer, break up any ice with a fork, beat mixture with electric mixer until ice crystals are broken up. Return to freezer until partially set and repeat.
4. Fold pecan nuts into ice-cream; pour back into loaf tin, cover with foil and freeze until set.

Serves 8

tip from the chef

For the pecan nuts to be crunchier, dry them in the oven at low temperature for 10 minutes.

the perfect
pavlova

■□□ | Cooking time: 2 hours - Preparation time: 15 minutes

method

1. Place egg whites in a mixing bowl and beat until soft peaks form. Gradually add sugar, beating well after each addition (a), until mixture is thick and glossy. Fold cornflour and vinegar into egg white mixture (b).
2. Grease a baking tray and line with nonstick baking paper. Grease paper and dust lightly with flour. Mark a 23 cm/9 in diameter circle on paper.
3. Place one quarter of the egg white mixture in the center of the circle (c) and spread out to within 3 cm/1¼ in of the edge. Pile remaining mixture around edge of circle and neaten using a metal spatula or knife.
4. Bake at 120°C/250°F/Gas ½ for 1½-2 hours or until firm to touch. Turn off oven and cool pavlova in oven with door ajar. Decorate cold pavlova with cream and top with fruit.

....

Serves 8

ingredients

> **6 egg whites**
> **1½ cups/315 g/10 oz caster sugar**
> **6 teaspoons cornflour, sifted**
> **1½ teaspoons white vinegar**
> **315 ml/10 oz cream, whipped**
> **selection of fresh fruits (orange segments, sliced bananas, sliced peaches, passion fruit pulp, berries, sliced kiwi fruits)**

tip from the chef

Both Australia and New Zealand claim to have created this truly marvelous dessert. However, both agree that it is named after the famous Russian ballerina.

a

b

c

passion
fruit pavlova

■□□ | Cooking time: 1 1/2 hour - Preparation time: 15 minutes

ingredients

> **6 egg whites, at room temperature**
> **pinch of cream of tartar**
> **2 teaspoons cornflour**
> **1 cup/250 g/8 oz caster sugar**
> **1¹/2 cups light cream, whipped**
> **4 passion fruits**
> **1 tablespoon fresh mint, cut into fine strips**

method

1. Beat egg whites with a handheld electric mixer until glossy. Combine cream of tartar, cornflour and sugar and gradually add to egg whites while motor is operating. Continue to beat for a further 5 minutes.
2. Grease and line the base and sides of a 23 cm/9 in springform tin with baking paper and lightly dust with cornflour, shake off any excess. Spoon meringue into prepared tin and spread top with knife to even out.
3. Bake at 130°C/260°F/Gas 1 for 1¹/2 hours. Turn off oven, leave door ajar and leave meringue to cool for 30 minutes. When cool, top with whipped cream, passion fruit and mint.

Serves 6-8

tip from the chef

Another option for topping the pavlova is to mix the whipped cream with raspberry purée and decorate with red fruits.

lemon
cheesecake

■□□ I Cooking time: 0 minute - Preparation time: 15 minutes

method

1. Place jelly crystals and gelatin in a bowl, pour over water and mix to dissolve. Cool to room temperature.
2. Place yogurt and cottage cheese in a food processor or blender and process until smooth. Add jelly mixture and process until combined.
3. Beat egg whites until soft peaks form, gently fold into cheese mixture. Pour mixture in a 20 cm/8 in springform tin, lined with plastic food wrap. Refrigerate until set.
4. Arrange strawberries on top of cheesecake. Garnish with blackberries on top and fresh mint sprigs around the base.

Serves 6

ingredients

> 3 tablespoons lemon jelly crystals
> 1 tablespoon gelatin
> 1 cup/250 ml/8 fl oz boiling water
> 2/3 cup/140 g/4 1/2 oz low-fat natural yogurt
> 1 cup/250 ml/8 fl oz low-fat cottage cheese
> 2 egg whites
> 120 g/4 oz strawberries, hulled and halved
> blackberries, to garnish
> fresh mint sprigs, to garnish

tip from the chef

Dissolve a little extra lemon jelly crystals in hot water, cool to room temperature and drizzle over strawberries.

World Wide Publication & Distribution:

STANDARD INTERNATIONAL MEDIA HOLDINGS

www.standardinternationalmedia.com

Chef Express Ultimate Collection Fresh Summer

Chef Express™ Best of Asia, Fresh Appetizers, Light & Easy Desserts, Seafood Splendor, Sensational Salads, Sizzling Barbecue

Publisher
Simon St. John Bailey

Editor-in-chief
Susan Knightley

Prepress
Precision Prep & Press

Printing
Tara TPS Korea

ISBN 9781600819773

2014